FAITHFUL FRIENDS

Holocaust Survivors' Stories
of the Pets who
Gave Them Comfort,
Suffered Alongside Them
and Waited for Their Return

"Could this be a subtle lesson of love
that God gives us through our pets?"

–Susan Bulanda in *God's Creatures*

FAITHFUL FRIENDS

Holocaust Survivors' Stories
of the Pets who
Gave Them Comfort,
Suffered Alongside Them
and Waited for Their Return

Compiled by
Susan Bulanda

CLADACH
Publishing

FAITHFUL FRIENDS : HOLOCAUST SURVIVORS' STORIES OF THE PETS WHO GAVE THEM COMFORT, SUFFERED ALONGSIDE THEM AND WAITED FOR THEIR RETURN
© 2011 Susan Bulanda
Published by Cladach Publishing, Greeley, CO 80634
www.cladach.com

Library of Congress Cataloging-in-Publication Data
Bulanda, Susan.
  Faithful friends : Holocaust survivors' stories of the pets who gave them comfort, suffered alongside them & waited for their return / compiled by Susan Bulanda.
       p. cm.
  Includes index.
  ISBN-13: 978-0-9818929-4-8
  ISBN-10: 0-9818929-4-9
  1. Pets--Social aspects. 2. Holocaust, Jewish (1939-1945)--Personal narratives. 3. Human-animal relationships--History--20th century. I. Title.
  SF416.B85 2011
  636.088'7--dc23

2011021452

ISBN-13: 978-0-9818929-4-8
Printed in the U.S.A.

Dedication

I have always had a desire to write and a love of writing. I can recall being very young lying on the floor by our front door, furiously writing a story. I continued to write stories which I did not share with anyone, until I reached junior high school (as it was called back in my day).

In ninth grade I had a wonderful English teacher, Miss Cecelia Spillane. She became my first inspiration, encouraging me to continue to write.

After I graduated high school, I met two wonderful people who became good friends and mentors, Marvin and Lois Greenberg. I shared with them my desire to be a published author and showed them my book of short stories. With their help I had my first piece of work published.

Therefore, I want to dedicate this book to the three people who inspired me and helped me become the writer I am today:

Miss Cecelia Spillane
and
Marvin and Lois Greenberg

Acknowledgments

I owe a hearty thank-you to all of the people who were willing to share their stories with me. Without them this book would not be possible. I also want to thank Catherine Lawton and her family of Cladach Publishing, for believing in this project. They published my last book, GOD'S CREATURES: A BIBLICAL VIEW OF ANIMALS, and were adventurous enough to trust me and take on this project. I also want to thank Michael Hanna-Fein, the editor of the Gantseh Megillah *for helping reach the people who made this book possible. Few authors can produce a book alone; it takes the help of many people to succeed. Thank you, all.*

I believe in the sun,
Even when it is not shining.
I believe in love,
Even when I am alone.
I believe in God,
Even when He is silent.

– inscription on a wall in Auschwitz,
author unknown

Foreword

This book has personal meaning for me since my uncle was a Holocaust survivor. Despite being terrorized by German shepherds while he was in a concentration camp, he made an immediate connection with dogs when he moved to America, an attachment that lasted a lifetime.

I also had a dear friend, Ursula Klau, who was a twelve-year-old child in the Bergen Belsen concentration camp. Her entire family grieved the pets that they were forced to leave behind. After being released from the camp, they learned that a family friend had saved the pets, keeping them for the rest of their lives. This knowledge was very healing for her and her family. She had dogs and cats for the rest of her life. What touched me the most was that she had a terrible fear of German shepherd dogs as a result of being frightened by the dogs at the concentration camp, and she let me help her overcome this fear. I recall the day when holding a soft-gentle Ger Shep puppy, she cried as she hugged the puppy, saying that she finally realized that the concentration dogs instinctively might have wanted to be gentle, but that they too had been horribly imprisoned by the Nazi armies.

Throughout my career working with many species of animals, I have witnessed and experienced the depth of the human-animal bond. As a certified animal behavior consultant and former president of the International Association of Animal Behavior Consultants, I have learned to appreciate the depth of intelligence that animals have as well as the bond that animals and people have for each other.

This book is the only book that captures both the human and animal side of the horrors that gripped the victims of the Holocaust—both those who suffered in the camps and those who were left behind. *Faithful Friends* is an important lesson for those who are too young to remember this time in history, and a reminder—hopefully providing closure—to those who do.

–Debbie Winkler
animal behaviorist, radio host, author

Table of Contents

INTRODUCTION ... 10

1. Hungary ... 16

Bogar by Kathy Rubin ... 18

Fliku by Irene Markley ... 32

2. Poland ... 41

Blackie by Annette Renschowicz ... 43

Ketzelah by Gloria Rubin ... 50

3. Belgium ... 63

The Cat by Jacob Stern ... 64

4. Holland ... 67

Hanni by Kurt Moses ... 69

Brady by Joyce Clemens ... 82

5. Romania ... 88

Jannet, Marcela & Cheelly by Lya Galperin ... 89

6. France ... 102

Nicolas by Yvonne Rothschild Klug (Redgis) ... 103

Nicolas, photo ... 108

Nicolas, pedigree ... 109

7. Yugoslavia ... 129

Dolly by Sonja Alaimo ... 130

Dolly, photo ... 132

ABOUT THE CONTRIBUTORS ... 139

SOURCES CONSULTED ... 142

INDEX ... 143

ABOUT THE AUTHOR ... 145

Introduction

The Holocaust was one of the most horrible events in recent history. Many books, articles and museums are dedicated to the Holocaust. But there is one more chapter of history to report—the experiences of the pets owned by the Holocaust victims.

Though I am not Jewish, I have always had a love and respect for God's chosen people. I have been fascinated by their history as told in the Bible. I realized early in life that without the Jewish people, there would be no Christians, since Jesus was Jewish. Marvin and Lois Greenberg, whom I met because of their German shepherd named Grindle, inspired and supported me at a time in my life when I had little other support. What I am today, I owe in large part to them.

In reading *The Diary of Anne Frank*, it struck me that these families in hiding risked their lives to bring a pet cat with them. They had to share their food with the cat, and to provide a litter box as well. They had to keep the cat quiet during the day. This made me wonder what happened to the other pets of the Holocaust victims.

I did not know how to find these pet-loving survivors; so I ran ads in Jewish publications. The person that helped me the most was Michael Hanna-Fein, editor of the *Gantseh Megillah* online magazine, in the "Together" section. I received a number of responses through this publication.

Some people may be puzzled by the topic of this book; yet every pet lover will realize that what happened to the victims of the Holocaust was in some way intensified by the fate of their pets. Some of the accounts are sad and some are happy; but all must be told.

As I researched this topic, survivors told me that they were glad someone cared enough to ask about their pets. They expressed to me that sharing their stories finally gave them closure—a testimony to how much their pets meant to them.

All accounts in this book are about the human-animal bond, and understanding that bond will help the reader appreciate the stories even more. Humans and animals have had a relationship since the beginning of time, but public understanding of this relationship did not emerge until the late 1800s when people began to protest animal cruelty. The book *Black Beauty* was an example of this emerging concern.

However, it was not until the late 1980s that the bond between people and their pets was recognized as such. Understanding the human-animal bond did not happen overnight; it has been a gradual process.

Even though the human-animal bond has only been "officially" recognized and studied in the past twenty to thirty years, today we have many organizations devoted to understanding the benefits of this bond, for both humans and animals. There are organizations such as the Delta Society and the International Society for Anthrozoology.

The human-animal bond runs so deep that concern

for the safety of a pet often prevents a person from leaving an abusive situation to go to a shelter, opting instead to risk their own life and/or physical well-being rather than abandon a pet to the whims of an abuser. Another example of this is when people refuse to be rescued from a natural disaster rather than leave their pet behind, often dying with the pet.

On the other side of this topic, there are accounts of animals who have risked their lives, in situations that were unnatural for the pet, to save their family. Animals have starved to death while mourning the loss of a human companion. Some accounts tell of an animal traveling hundreds of miles to return home.

Modern research has shown that assistance and therapy dogs, or even the mere presence of animals will lower a human's blood pressure. Pets are useful tools in reaching children with mental and physical disorders. The results are sometimes remarkable, such as in the case of some autistic children, the mentally ill and the elderly. Pets often give the lonely, isolated or introverted person a positive connection. Pets can open the door for social contact and friendships with other pet-loving people.

Today we know that there are medical and psychological benefits associated with a positive relationship to our pets. However, during World War II, this was still uncharted territory. Nevertheless, the bond existed and people suffered loss, hurt and cried over their pets. They cared beyond what words can describe.

At that time there were no support groups or sympathy given for those who mourned the loss of a pet. Many people were afraid to say anything or make a big deal about it in light of what happened to humans, and this hindered their grieving process.

Yet, without exception, every person who shared his or her story in this collection said they felt glad that they could do so. Keep in mind that the people who were able to tell me firsthand about their experiences, were children at the time of the Holocaust—children who did not fully understand the political climate, why their lives became a nightmare, or why their pets had to be left behind.

Although, for ease of reading and understanding, I have added some details and dialog to the accounts in this book, all of the accounts are true to what was told to me. Some names have been added or changed, and the feelings of the animals themselves were fictionalized by me based on my knowledge of animal behavior.

Holocaust Timeline

▶1879-1880: Heinrich von Treitschke, a popular German nationalist historian, coins the phrase *Die Juden sind unser Unglück* which means "The Jews are our misfortune." This becomes the slogan on Nazi banners. Journalist Wilhelm Marr coins the phrase *anti-Semitism*.

▶1933: The Nazi state begins. In January, Adolf Hitler becomes the Chancellor of Germany. National boycott of Jewish businesses and laws are formed to push the Jews out of German society.

▶1934: German President Paul von Hindenburg dies and Hitler becomes the unchallenged leader of Germany. New laws are passed that ban and eradicate more Jews from schools and the professions.

▶1935: Nueremberg Laws are passed, allowing only Germans and those related to Germans to be German citizens. German Jews become non-citizens or stateless. The military overtakes Saarland.

▶1936: Signs stating "Jews are unwanted here" are removed for the summer Olympics but restored as soon as the games are over.

▶1937: Jewish merchants lose their businesses without justification.

▶1938: November riots result in "The Night of Broken Glass." Many Jews are killed or injured. Austria is annexed, bringing 190,000 more Jews under German rule.

▶1939: WWII starts with the invasion of Poland. SS Security Chief Reinhard Hydrich declares that all Polish Jews will be confined to ghettos.

▶1943: The Warsaw uprising is led by Mordecai Anielewicz, who forms the Zydowska Organizacja Bojowa, (ZOB Jewish Fighting Organization). This event inspires other resistance groups and instills some fear in the Nazis.

▶1945: May, the end of WWII

▶1946: Nuremberg Trial of Nazi war criminals

▶1948: The Jewish National Council proclaims the state of Israel.

Memories of People and their Pets
from Hungary, Poland, Belgium,
Holland, Romania, France
and Yugoslavia

1. HUNGARY

Even years before WWII, the political climate of Hungary was not positive toward the Jewish people. In July 1920, Count Pál Teleki was appointed Prime Minister and his right-wing government passed laws that limited "political insecure elements," which often meant Jews, from entering universities. The radical counterrevolutionaries continued to terrorize Jews and "leftists" into the next regime, under Count István Bethlen. However, Count István Bethlen did put a stop to their activities and restored order to the country.

Unfortunately, around 1932, a new prime minister, Gyula Gömbös, changed the climate in Hungary, collaborated with Germany and became dependent upon Germany for raw materials and markets. Hitler pressured the Hungarian government into supporting Nazism.

Kálmán Darányi, who succeeded Gömbös, tried to appease both the Nazis and anti-Semites by passing the "First Jewish Law" which limited the number of Jews allowed into certain professions to twenty percent. Following Darányi, Béla Imrédy became Prime Minister and instituted "The Second Jewish Law" which restricted Jewish employment and more importantly, classified Jews as a race instead of a religion.

June 26, 1941 Hungary declared war, entering WWII. The Hungarian army succeeded in the Battle of Uman, on the Eastern Front. However, by 1943 the Second Hungarian army suffered at the River Don, causing the government to try to negotiate surrender with the Allies. This did not agree with the Germans. Very quietly, on March 19, 1944, they marched into and occupied Hungary. This march was known as Operation Margarethe. Thus Hungary became a German satellite.

Between May and June of 1944, the political Arrow Cross Party, dedicated to anti-Semitism, and the Hungarian police deported over 440,000 Jews to Auschwitz. Of these, only 40,000 Hungarian Jews survived. The Germans also murdered tens of thousands of Romani people as well as hundreds of Hungarian people who sheltered Jews.

On February 13, 1945, Hungary surrendered unconditionally. On May 8, 1945, WWII ended.

After the adoption of anti-Jewish laws, Jews were forbidden to join the military but were "drafted" into the Munkaszolgálat or the Hungarian Labor Service System (HLSS). They were forced to work in the mines, in construction, and to clear mine fields. The members of the HLSS were often mistreated by Jewish-hating Hungarian officers—denied boots, food and often tortured by being doused with water in the dead of winter and forced to stand still until the water turned to ice. They were also forced to play games and perform acrobatics to amuse the Hungarian officers. Nevertheless, when the Germans occupied Hungary in 1944, many Jews were able to save themselves from deportation by doing hard labor in the HLSS.

Many other Jews in the HLSS lost their lives as casualties of war, partly because Russian captors considered them enemies. And soon after the first anti-Semitic laws took effect, the mass murdering of Jews began. In July and August of 1941 over 16,000 Jews were deported to a territory under German rule, where they were slaughtered. Then in January 1942 the Hungarians murdered 3,500 people, of which at least 800 were Jews. They simply tossed the bodies of the murdered people into the Danube River.

Bogar

by Kathy Rubin

One special day in 1939 my father came home from work and called to us, "Children, children! Come see what Papa brought home!" We all ran to my father, excited. On occasion my father would bring home a special treat for us, such as our favorite bread or a cheese round and sometimes sweets.

As we ran to my father to see what he had brought, we did not see a package in his hand. We did not see anything. My father was smiling his biggest smile, so we knew that he must have something. Then Father's coat wiggled and from under it a little black nose appeared.

"Papa, Papa, what is it?" We all asked, my big sister jumping up and down and clapping her hands. We couldn't wait and grabbed at my father's coat to get it open. Nestled against his warmth was a small, furry puppy. My father took the little ball of black fluff from his coat and handed it to us. We all wanted to pet and hold it. We sat on the floor and took turns cuddling the puppy.

His eyes were like liquid chocolate and he gave

us little kisses as he wiggled from one to the other. My mother had come into the room to see what all of the excitement was. She did not say much, but I saw her glance at my father with the look that said, "What have you done?"

My mother sighed as my father shrugged his shoulders and gave her a look that said, "I couldn't help it."

We named the puppy Bogar, and it did not take long for all five of us—my parents, older brother, sister, and me—to fall in love with him. We loved to hold him and bury our faces in his soft, shiny fur. Bogar even won my mother's affection. After all, how could you resist such a bundle of love?

Bogar did many funny things that made us laugh. One time he decided that my father's pants made a good toy and grabbed onto them as my father tried to walk out the door. We all laughed so hard, we could not get Bogar to stop. After that we all tried to get Bogar to grab my father's pants legs when he walked through the room. Bogar, however, was smarter than we were; he knew my father did not find this pastime amusing.

Another time when we were all outside playing, Bogar saw a butterfly and started to chase it. The butterfly flew in circles and Bogar tripped over his own feet chasing it round and round. We rolled on the ground laughing, then imitated him by twisting our legs and falling over.

Bogar had a keen sense of smell. If we were outside, he would alert us as soon as my mother started to cook or bake a special treat. His favorite meal was dinner, since he always got a scrap of meat or other leftovers.

Although there was an undercurrent of tension in our community in Hajduhadhaz, Hungary (Hajdúhadház is a town in the Hajdú-Bihar county, in the Northern Great Plain region of Hungary) due to the anti-Semitic feelings and the war that had started, Bogar brought us happiness and joy. When we played with him, we entered a trouble-free world of love and joy. It was comforting to snuggle with Bogar. Often all of us kids would lie prone in the shade of a big tree, on the grass in the summer with Bogar next to us and make up stories or share a story from one of our books. These were some of the best times.

Bogar never grew big; he weighed only twenty pounds. He was all black and of undetermined heritage, but we loved him. He seemed to sense our trials and would rest his little head on an arm or leg, or curl up in a lap, sometimes sleeping or just gazing into our eyes. All of us would wonder what he was thinking, and what did he feel?

He made us laugh and was a constant source of joy, amusement and companionship to us. Sometimes, as my mother sat in her favorite chair to read a book, Bogar would jump up into her lap and fall asleep. He especially liked to do this when the weather was cold or wet outside.

I, especially, bonded with Bogar. He followed me everywhere. Many times he and I would sit together alone and I would tell him all of my secrets.

I remember one time when we heard bombs in the distance. My parents were frightened and could not hide their fear from us. That night I hid Bogar in my bed, under the covers with me. Somehow, he made me less afraid. We kids would hear stories about the war. And even though our parents and other grown-ups would not talk about it in front of us or within our hearing, they could not hide from us the worried looks and tense whispers that passed between them.

My friends and I would have our secret meetings and share the rumors we heard through the children's grapevine, as well as bits of conversations that we overheard. Those of us who had dogs would include them in our secret meetings. Somehow their presence made us feel safer.

Our family managed to survive the first five years of the war because Hungary did not enter the war until March, 1944. However, the war affected us all; for example, my father was taken several times into forced labor in the Hungarian Military starting in 1943.

Even Bogar hated the sound of planes and shooting. Before we could hear it, Bogar would growl and raise the hair on his back when an airplane flew near.

Then the unthinkable happened, the thing we all feared. In June of 1944, we heard a commotion outside. On a loud speaker the soldiers told all Jews to line up in the street. My parents had told us that this might happen and not to be afraid.

We had no place to run to or to hide. The soldiers came into the houses and told everyone to get ready to leave. We were only allowed to take one suitcase each. We rushed to grab some clothes and a few other things as the soldiers waved their rifles threateningly at us. We heard shots fired in the distance.

I saw my friends—our neighbors, the butcher, the doctor, and the banker—all of the people I grew up knowing and loving. They were standing, cowering and crying, in the street. There were young people, middle-aged people, and the elderly trying to stand on feeble legs with help from their relatives. Way down at the end of the line I heard a man yelling. Then I heard shots. I was afraid to look. It got very quiet after that; people talked in whispers.

As soon as we were lined up in the street, we were marched to the ghetto. We had no warning and no time to make provisions for ourselves or Bogar. We only had time to leave Bogar free outside. I prayed to God that he would be safe. But to my horror, when I looked around, I saw that Bogar was following us to the ghetto!

"Go home!" I cried. "Go home, Bogar." But he did not. Dogs were not allowed in the ghetto, so as we passed through the gates, the soldiers chased Bogar, trying to hit him. I tried to run back to him, but my father held me by the arm and forced me to stay. I had never felt so helpless.

I thought I heard Bogar yelp, but I could not be sure since I could not see him, and we had no idea where he was or what was happening to him. Though afraid and uncertain about our own fate, we also worried about Bogar. Who would take care of him? How would he survive?

For three weeks we were kept in the ghetto in Hajduhadhaz where we lived in someone's small summer home. After three weeks we were again lined up in the street. We were herded out of the ghetto and forced to walk to the train station in Hajduhadhaz.

I looked around as I left the ghetto. I am not sure whether I wanted to see Bogar or was hoping that he would be gone. But I couldn't stop from looking. And as we left the ghetto, to our surprise, Bogar was right there beside us. My dear, sweet Bogar had waited outside of the ghetto for us.

Initially I was thrilled to see that he was alive, but when he followed us all the way to the train station, my heart sank. I couldn't help the tears that fell down my face. I anguished over what Bogar would do. Would he follow the train? Would he be killed under the wheels of the train? Would someone shoot him? Poor Bogar did not know we would have to leave him again. What would happen to our precious dog? All I could think of was Bogar, not even about myself. Maybe by thinking of Bogar I was able to handle my deeper fears. We had all heard stories about the camps.

Bogar did not understand what was happening. He watched his family line up and march with everyone else. He had often gone on walks with his people; perhaps this was a walk of some kind. But he could smell the fear and sense the tension, so he knew it wasn't a family outing like before.

When his loved ones went into the ghetto, the guards shooed him away. When he would not leave and tried to get inside to be with his family, they threw stones at him that hurt him so badly he yelped. He quickly learned not to linger near the gate. He had been left at home before, but his family had always come back, and it was rare for everyone to be gone at the same time.

So Bogar waited outside the gates of the ghetto for his family to return, being careful to stay far enough away so that no one paid much attention to him. Every now and then a soldier would toss him some scraps to eat. There was a stream nearby where he was able to drink water, and when it rained he had the puddles.

After what seemed like a lifetime, Bogar saw

people coming out of the gates in a long line. He ran up and down the line until he found them, his people. Then he jumped and wiggled with joy—now they would all go home!

But they did not go home. They marched again. So, being a loyal dog, Bogar followed them.

Finally they reached the train station and he saw his family climb into a big square train car with lots of other people. There was crying. Occasionally a gun shot made him cringe; the hair rose up on his back and a deep growl rumbled in his throat.

Again, he was forced apart from his family. The soldiers shouted and shoved people. Once in a while a boot would swing in Bogar's direction. The people getting on the train did not pay attention to him and he had to run a distance away to avoid being trampled. As he hid in some bushes, he whimpered softly, sensing that his people were going far away, leaving him for good.

Once everyone was gone, he slowly wandered around trying to figure out what had happened. He was hungry, thirsty and tired. At first he ran after the train; but he could not catch up to it. Next he went back to the ghetto, hoping that he would find his people and food there, but gone were the few soldiers who had been kind to him. He headed back to his home.

Time passed, and he found it harder to get food. There were no food scraps in the streets or garbage heaps. One time he went up to a man and the man grabbed him and hurt him. He bit the man and got away, but he instinctively knew that the man would have killed him. He became fearful of all people and avoided them, running each time someone saw him or hiding when he detected them first.

Things were not much better when he got back to his home. Some of the neighbors who were still there and knew him would leave a scrap of bone for him or some rotted food. He was not accustomed to eating vegetables but he was so hungry that he ate anything he could find. Once he even chewed the soles of a boot that he found. He went from being a clean dog with a shiny coat to a dirty, matted dog whose ribs stuck out. Even the rats, rabbits and mice became scarce. Once in a while he would catch a bird and would even eat bugs. The days wore on.

Our family survived the next year in Grafenegg, Austria, where I worked in forced labor doing farm work. After that we were sent to Theresienstadt in Czecholslovakia. We had little to eat and lived in horrible conditions. During the first few weeks we would complain to our parents that we were hungry. But we quickly realized that everyone was hungry and that there was nothing we could do. We had to guard our meager possessions and food carefully. We stayed together for protection because other people would steal our food or clothes if we were not careful. Life in the camp was a constant fight for survival.

We were never personally threatened. But we heard rumors that caused us to wonder from day to day whether we would be shot or tortured. And we all prayed for Bogar. It helped me to think of him instead of myself. I would curl up under my coat and pretend he was there for me to hold and tell secrets to. In my mind I would relive the fun times we used to have together. Thoughts of Bogar gave me hope.

Then on May 5, 1945 we were herded to the middle of the camp. This was not unusual, since the guards would check to see that no one had escaped, and to remove the bodies of those who had died in the night. But this time a murmur, an excitement moved through the line. I did not understand and was too weak to care very much anymore. If it had not been for the hope of seeing Bogar again, I would rather have given up and died. At least I would not be hungry or cold anymore. But I had promised Bogar that I would come back for him.

This time, on that glorious day in May, 1945, we were free! We were herded up and sent out to fend for ourselves, but we were free. We were alive and all of my family had survived. We started the long walk back to our home. It was the only place we could go.

I'll never forget walking that final mile. Because we were all so weak, we did not talk. But in our hearts, we wondered if Bogar would be there for us. I saw my parents and sister and brother look around as we got closer. I strained my eyes to see if I could spot Bogar. How I wished he would be there for us. How I missed him and wanted to hold him, tell him all that had happened, tell him that I really had not wanted to leave him, and that we were sorry. I wanted to cry into his soft, comforting fur.

We drew closer and closer to home, but no Bogar. No happy bark, no wiggling puppy, no soft fur. When we reached our house we settled into what was left of our home. People had ransacked it looking for food, stealing anything they wanted. But at least we had a roof over our head, a stove to cook on and beds to sleep in. Some of our clothes were left, and some of our household goods. We needed everything that was left in order to survive. We established a routine of looking for food and fuel, and putting our lives back together.

"Papa," my sister, brother and I asked, "do you think Bogar will come home?"

"Dear children" he replied, "we will pray for him and keep hoping, but I want you all to be happy that we are all here. God will take care of Bogar."

We all still longed for Bogar. Our home didn't feel the same without him.

Every day I would walk around our community, hoping to see Bogar, praying that God would bring him home to me and my family. I asked everyone I met if they had seen him, but most people were not sure; they did not remember what he looked like. They were busy trying to survive and did not pay much attention to stray dogs. Many dogs roamed the area. Some people I asked thought Bogar was dead, others thought they saw him run away. This was understandable, since they may have seen him follow us to the ghetto and thought he was gone.

The days passed and I could not find him. I was not strong enough to walk far or I would have walked back to the ghetto and train station to look for him. Slowly my hopes diminished. We were all thankful that we made it through the war and that we were still alive. We were joyful to be reunited with some of our neighbors and friends and to be able to worship at the synagogue again. But we mourned the loss of one family member: Bogar.

We had heard stories of dogs being caught and eaten, or being beaten or shot by soldiers. The bigger dogs would attack the smaller dogs as they starved to death. It wrenched my heart to hear these stories. I kept thinking that Bogar hated the sounds of war and the soldiers so much that he would try to escape. But how could he find food? I knew that, to survive, people had caught and eaten all the animals they could get. I wondered, *What will be left for Bogar?* Then I remembered that he was small and he would not need much food to live.

A month later, I was walking down the road

about a mile from home, still hoping to find Bogar when I saw a dog that looked like Bogar. I thought my eyes were playing tricks on me. My heart skipped a beat and I held my breath. I was so afraid to call his name because I was sure it would not be him and it would hurt so much if it wasn't.

Hesitantly, I called out, "Bogar! Bogar!"

The dog stopped and looked, frozen in place. Then like a shooting star, he ran to me, jumping and licking my hands and face. It was Bogar, my sweet, wonderful Bogar!

I knelt down and hugged him for a long time. I felt so happy and relieved. I thanked God for taking care of him. For the first time since we were taken away, I felt peace and hope. God did care.

The two of us hurried home as fast as our weak bodies could, and I burst through the door shouting to the family, "Bogar's home! Bogar's home!"

We all hugged and kissed him, then we all hugged each other, tears in everyone's eyes. Next we gave him some of our precious little food, water and a soft, warm place to sleep. After we got over our excitement, we saw that Bogar had had a rough life while we were gone. He was thin, his coat did not shine, and it seemed that there was a haunted look in his eyes.

The next day I started to ask people if they had seen Bogar in the past year. When some people saw him they remembered. We found out from people in our neighborhood that he had lived on the street, stealing food when he could.

For the next year we had our wonderful Bogar with us. Then when he was a little over seven years of age, he got sick and died. It meant a lot to us that for one glorious year our family was complete. When Bogar died, we all mourned deeply.

Fliku

by Irene Markley

I was born in 1925 in Munkacs, Hungary, the youngest of eleven children. In 1940 our neighbor's dog had a litter of puppies. Father went to see the tiny puppies and fell in love with one little guy. These were small fox terriers—good ratters and not too big—so they would not eat much. Since my father liked the one special puppy, our neighbors gave him that one. Father named the puppy *Fliku,* and they became inseparable.

Each morning my father would say, "Come, Fliku, it is time to go to synagogue." Fliku knew the routine because they went every morning. It was a familiar sight in our town to see Fliku sitting in front of the synagogue as my father, who was very Orthodox, went to worship.

Each morning as Father climbed the synagogue stairs, he would say, "Fliku, now you stay here, no noise, you pray and wait for me." Fliku would look at him as if he understood and would sit or lie in the sun. Fliku never strayed, but waited patiently for his master outside the synagogue.

When Father came out of the synagogue, he would say, "Good boy! Now let's go to the market." Fliku would bark and jump for joy. For a little dog he could jump very high. Then Father and Fliku would go to the Jewish street where he would buy meat or fish for the day. Fliku loved this part because he always got a small piece of fish or meat from the butcher. Sometimes he also got a stale crust from the baker.

As they walked to and from the market, Father would stop and chat with neighbors and friends. Fliku always enjoyed playing with children, who would throw sticks for him. When the children hugged him, they received dog kisses on their cheeks. When a child was not feeling well, Fliku would cuddle with them as if he wanted to make them feel better. The children loved this so much that they would often pretend not to feel well to get Fliku to cuddle with them. They would see him coming and start to complain. "Oh, I do not feel well." "Oh, my back aches." One might hold her tummy and say, "Oh, I have a belly ache." I think Fliku knew they were pretending in order to get him to cuddle with them, but he played along with them anyway. I think he got a good laugh from the antics. During these visits, many of the grownups would bend over to pat him; he was such a friendly dog.

Father and Fliku were a familiar sight around town, beloved by all. One of the reasons why Father was liked so much was because he was always cheerful and took the time to talk to people. Fliku was always ready to wag his tail or give a child kisses on the cheek. It was hard to think of my father apart from the dog; the two of them seemed like one.

Fliku loved to play and would invent games if we would not play with him. Several times a day he would try to lure us into a game.

I recall one time when my mother and I were in our yard tending our small garden and we heard Fliku whine.

"Fliku" my mother said, "I cannot play with you now."

Fliku was quiet for a moment, and then he whined again. My mother said, "I told you I cannot—" she turned around and then started to laugh. Fliku had our elderly neighbor's bloomers between his paws!

"Oh!" My mother gasped and grabbed the frilly underwear. Fliku looked delighted, his eyes full of laughter. I did not want to go to the neighbor's house with my mother to return the bloomers. I was too embarrassed. I never learned how he got ahold of that particular garment.

This was not unusual for Fliku to do; he was a little devil at times with his mischief. If he took something from a neighbor's yard, we would laugh and return it. Neighbors always thought it was funny too. Fliku never chewed or destroyed anything; and his antics often gave me, my mother, and the neighbors a chance to visit and take a quick break from the daily chores.

Fliku would bring us anything he could find and could carry, for us to throw. He was a busy dog and liked to be active most of the time. Fliku brought joy to all of us with his funny escapades and affectionate companionship.

But as funny as Fliku was, he couldn't take our minds off the fears of what would happen when the Germans came. We did not know exactly what to expect. Many in our community believed that, when and if the Germans did come, they would do no more than force us to live under their rules and restrictions until the war ended. However, my one brother did not believe this is what would happen; he had heard rumors of murder and forced labor. So before the Germans came, he fled to Budapest where he lived under a Christian name.

Then, the day we all feared finally came. I will never forget it. The German soldiers made all the Jewish people—about half the town—line up in the street. We trembled with fright.

The Germans told us to go home and pack a few belongings. They gave us very little time.

While my mother packed, my father took Fliku back to the neighbors where he had been born. Father hoped Fliku would remember them and be happy to stay there until we returned. None of us believed that we would be gone for long.

We did what the Germans ordered us to do because, even though we were all frightened, we did not want to get into trouble.

Within half an hour after we started walking to the ghetto, my father felt a little body press against his leg. When he looked down he saw it was Fliku.

"Go home! Go home!" my father said. I could hear the sadness in his voice. But Fliku would not leave him. My father was wearing a long coat so he picked up Fliku, hiding the little dog under the coat. He told Fliku, "Now stay still and quiet." Fliku did not move or make a sound. I think he understood.

We went to live with an aunt who lived in the ghetto. Since dogs were not allowed in the ghetto, we hid Fliku in my aunt's house with us for a day while we settled in. The gates of the ghetto were opened—we could come in and go out at will—so we took Fliku back to the neighbor who gave him to us. We knew Fliku would be safe with these Christian people. We hoped that this time Fliku would remember them and know to stay there.

When we left, Fliku paced in the house, barked and would not settle down. Looking back on those times, I think that he knew this situation was not good and that he wanted nothing else but to be with my father. The neighbor tried to keep Fliku from running after us, but he would not settle down. By the time night came, the neighbor tethered him so he could not run away. The neighbors cared about Fliku and wanted what was best for him.

The very next morning we heard barking outside the ghetto gate. My sister and I went to look and there was Fliku with a bloody neck.

"Oh no, Fliku, Father is going to be very mad at you," we said as we hugged him. My sister cried when she saw the blood on his neck. We were both afraid the Germans would get angry with Fliku and shoot him or beat him. Trying to keep him hidden, we carried Fliku back to my aunt's house.

My father was upset, but he cleaned Fliku and dressed his wound as best as he could, then took him back to the neighbor. When we asked what had happened, they told us that he was so restless that they tied him to keep him home. Fliku pulled so much that he hurt his neck before he finally escaped.

We all noticed that Fliku seemed to be different after these two adventures. Perhaps the soldiers had hit or kicked him. He was not the happy dog we had known. But we were too overwhelmed with other happenings to give much thought to this at the time.

My father had a sadness I had rarely seen in his face as he told Fliku, "My little boy, you need to stay here. I will be back for you as soon as I can." Fliku seemed to know what he was talking about and looked very upset. My father picked him up and held him close to his face. I could see the tears on his cheeks as Fliku tried to kiss them away. I thought his hands shook a bit as he handed Fliku to the neighbors. I wondered why he was so upset when we all felt that we would return home soon, that the Germans would not keep us for long.

With a dog's sense of the situation, Fliku knew that the German soldiers were the cause of his being separated from his beloved family. He could see and feel the sadness and fear in his family. His instinct was to protect his loved ones, but he was not allowed to do this. He would have given his life for them.

He remembered the family that bred and raised him for the first months of his life, and he loved them too, but his heart was with Father. He realized that his family had moved and he knew where they were.

Being an obedient dog, he understood the second time he was brought back to his breeder's house that Father wanted him to stay there, just as he had understood he was to wait outside the synagogue when Father went in to pray. He felt restless, though, and for days Fliku cried and paced. He could not help his broken heart.

The neighbors noticed that when he curled up into a little ball to sleep, he would often tremble as if he was having bad dreams. And they noticed how dramatically he changed. Every time a soldier passed he would snarl and bark. At first he did this from a distance, but over time he got bolder. The neighbors tried to keep him from doing it, but there was no consoling Fliku. The neighbors were fighting for survival as well. Food was scarce. Fliku's rage increased until he would run up to any soldier he saw and bite at their pants legs. Fliku's anger grew by the day.

We were not aware of what was happening to Fliku because the times were tense and there was talk that we would be sent to the concentration camps. We assumed that, because he had not run away again, Fliku must have settled down and was OK.

My family made plans for my sister and me to follow my brother to Budapest. So the next day I escaped to travel to Budapest where I lived under a Christian name; and shortly after, my sister did the same. Then one day I was caught by German soldiers on the train and put in another town. However, I escaped a second time.

The rest of my family died in Auschwitz.

After the war, I returned to my hometown. There I met the man who would become my husband. I tried to look for Fliku but the times were hard and I did not have much time to look for him. We moved to a displaced persons' camp in Hungary where we lived for four years. In 1949 we went to America.

I never forgot Fliku and could not stop thinking about him and wondering what happened to him. In

1989 I went back to my hometown in Hungary to find out what I could about Fliku.

I learned that after my family went to the ghetto Fliku "went wild" and hated anyone in a uniform. He would attack them, biting their pants legs.

The more Fliku saw soldiers the more hostile he got, attacking them at every chance he could. Finally a Hungarian soldier shot and killed Fliku. The neighbor took his broken little body and buried it in our yard.

I cried from the bottom of my heart, even though I knew that had he lived his life to full expectancy, he would have been dead of natural causes by now. I guess I had hoped that Fliku had settled in his new home and had a long, happy life. The thought of Fliku being so distraught added to the grief of losing my family.

I asked the people who lived in our house if we could go in the yard to see where he was buried. But they were not sympathetic and would not let me go into the yard to do that. I still ache in my heart when I think of Fliku; he was so much a part of my father and our family, of our community and the happiness that we once knew.

2. POLAND

World War II started with the invasion of Poland by the German Army on September 1, 1939. The Russian invasion of eastern Poland on September, 17, 1939 destroyed any hope the Polish people had of fighting back on a conventional level. Poland's Western allies, England and France, then declared war on Germany on September 3, 1939.

Hitler fully believed that he would be able to take over Poland without any military response from Britain and France. The Germans did not think they would suffer losses. However, they lost 16,000 troops and about thirty percent of their armored vehicles. The Polish people lost 65,000 troops.

Almost immediately, the Polish government exiled to France and formed a new Polish army of about 80,000 men known as the Polish Highland Brigade, which fought in the Battle of Norway. The First Grenadier Division and the Second Infantry Fusiliers Division helped to defend France. These were just a few of the Polish divisions and squadrons that took part in WWII.

It is interesting that Poland, with its government in exile, never surrendered to Germany; and the Polish people were instrumental in helping the Allies fight the war.

The Polish resistance, called the Armia Krajowa (Home Army) numbered 200,000 to 300,000 soldiers, plus many sympathizers. There was also an under-

ground ultra-nationalist force called Narodowe Sily Zbrojne (National Armed Forces). Other resistance groups were also organized by the Polish Jews.

In Poland Hitler began his plan to concentrate, remove and eliminate all Jews from Europe.

The German Wehreacht or Armed Forces, were responsible for the murder of many Jewish people. For example, in October of 1941, the Wehreacht drowned thirty Jewish children in clay pits near the Okopowa Street in the Warsaw Ghetto. Between September and October 1941, 20,000 Jews were murdered by the SS in the eastern provinces of Poland.

However, the Auschwitz death camps were where the most Jewish people were killed. Auschwitz was established in 1940, mostly for Polish political prisoners. Auschwitz eventually was made up of three camps, Auschwitz I or the main camp, Auschwitz II or Birkenau, and Auschwitz III or Buna-Monowitz. Auschwitz II, which had an assembly-line style of extermination, was the top killing center. There were four crematoria which the Germans boasted could incinerate up to 4500 bodies a day.

During the years 1943 and 1944, hundreds of thousands of Jewish people were killed, either by starvation, forced labor, disease or extermination.

The entire Auschwitz operation (three camps) had five crematoria and killed over a million Jews.

Blackie

by Annette Renschowicz

When I was young, we lived in Poland in a hamlet near the city of Czestochowa. Life was pleasant for a young girl. My grandparents lived on a farm in a hamlet near Czestochowa as well and we would often visit and play with the animals.

On one visit to the farm my grandfather said to me, "Annette, come look at what I have."

We walked into the barn and entered a stall. In the straw, curled up, was the cutest puppy—black with a white collar.

"Oh, Grandpa, what a sweet puppy he is and so cute!" I exclaimed as I sat in the straw next to him.

He had soft eyes and kissed my face and wiggled every time I held him. We called him Blackie. Grandfather had another dog, Farmisht, and the two dogs would play together. Blackie loved to play "Catch me if you can" with Farmisht. He would run in circles around Farmisht and then the two of them would dash off in a gleeful jaunt. But mostly Farmisht was a farm dog and was very close to Grandfather. He would follow Grandfather around the farm as he worked, helping when he was needed.

Tension between Jews and non-Jews was becoming a problem in our hamlet. Non-Jews would taunt and snub their Jewish friends. One day I was walking down the lane with Blackie when some children came over to us.

"Hi!" I called out, hoping that they would play with me. These were children that I knew and had played with before, but I quickly saw that their faces were angry.

"Jew pig!" they yelled at me and called me other names. They continued to taunt me and then one boy picked up a rock and threw it. I ducked but heard a horrible yelp from Blackie. When the children heard the yelp, they ran away. I rushed over to Blackie. He was bleeding. I started to cry and carried him home as fast as I could.

The rock had hit Blackie in the eye. My mother tended to Blackie but he lost the sight in that eye. Despite that, he was a friendly dog who loved to play.

It was 1940; times were getting hard and food was becoming scarce. My family now lived on the farm with Grandfather. It was easier that way to survive. Often relatives would come to the farm from the city of Czestochowa to get some food and to visit. The tension in the city was mounting and it was a joy for everyone to visit on the farm. While we were all together, for a short time it seemed like the war was far away and we were happy again. I loved living on the farm and being around the farm animals. I liked to help in the garden and learn to cook from my mother and grandmother.

One day my grandfather's nephew, Joel, who was fifteen, came for a visit from the city of Czestochowa where his family lived in an apartment. They had come often to visit and Joel had fallen in love with Blackie. Blackie had taken to Joel as well.

On one visit Joel pleaded, "Grandfather, I love Blackie, would you give him to me? Please, Grandpa, please?"

Our grandfather thought a few minutes. He knew that life in the city was getting worse and that Joel was suffering the loss of friends, just as we were. He thought that Blackie might make Joel's life a little better and give him some companionship and happiness.

"Joel, we all love Blackie, but it is getting hard to feed two dogs because the leftovers are becoming scarce. If you promise to take care of him and you think you can feed him, then OK."

Joel was ecstatic; and as time passed, he and Blackie became fast friends. Wherever Joel went, the dog went too.

Months later, Joel and his father were sitting in the kitchen when suddenly Blackie's ears perked up and he stared at the window. The next instant he ran out of the room. Joel followed him to see what he was doing and was surprised to find him hiding under his bed. Joel's father said, "Someone is coming from the farm in the hamlet and the dog knows."

In about fifteen minutes they heard a knock on the door. When Joel answered it, he saw my grandfather standing at the door.

"Grandfather!" Joel said, excited. "You will never guess what happened. Blackie ran and hid under the bed and Papa said it was because someone was coming from the hamlet."

"Let me see," said Grandfather, and he walked into the bedroom and looked under the bed. Sure enough, Blackie was hiding.

"Blackie, come out here, boy," Grandfather said. But Blackie would not come out from under the bed. The bed was against a wall and he was far under the bed with his head in the corner of the wall.

"I know you are angry with me because I gave you away," Grandfather told Blackie. "But we had to do it so that you would eat and Joel would have a friend."

Later, after my grandfather left, Joel was standing in the kitchen when he felt something lean against his leg. It was Blackie, who was his happy self again.

"Father," Joel said. "You were right, and Grandfather was right; Blackie was angry with him." They both had a good laugh over this.

The war continued to intensify and food became even scarcer in the city. One day after he was done with his chores, Joel noticed that Blackie was not in the house. He asked his parents if they had seen him but they had not. It was still early in the day so he decided to look for Blackie.

"I am going to search around the neighborhood," Joel told his parents.

"OK, but be careful. Do not get in trouble and stay away from the soldiers."

Joel searched all of the streets and alleyways, asking everyone he saw, until darkness fell and it became too hard to see. Sad and worried he went home and sat slumped in the kitchen chair, staring at the floor. Joel's father felt very bad for his son because he knew how much he loved Blackie.

"Joel," his father said, "did you go upstairs to the top apartment to see if those neighbors have seen Blackie?"

"No, Papa, I didn't. Do you think he could be up there?" Joel asked, recovering hope. The people upstairs had children, and Blackie loved children. Maybe they let him come in to play. Joel rushed up the stairs, praying that they had seen Blackie and knew where he was.

Breathlessly he knocked on the door. The house-wife answered. Joel asked, "Have you seen my dog Blackie?"

"Yes," the woman told him. "I know where your dog is. We are so hungry that we killed him and are cooking him in the stew pot!"

Joel turned around wordlessly and went back to his apartment and cried. He did not have much time to mourn, though, because a short time later all Jews in the area were marched to the ghetto, including our entire family. Grandfather left Farmisht free on the farm, hoping he would survive. We did not have time to do anything else for the animals.

We feared what would happen to us and what would happen to our beloved animals.

Farmisht did not understand the turmoil that was happening. His family met many other people in the street, and then they began walking away. Often when Grandfather would go to market he would leave Farmisht behind to wait on the front steps of the house until he returned. This time Grandfather ordered Farmisht to stay behind as he had done so often. Farmisht knew his job was to watch the farm and he tried to do that. But people came and stole the few chickens that were left and raided the garden. People also went into the house and took things. He was not an aggressive dog; all he did was jump and bark. Finally there was nothing left to watch. Then somehow he understood that his family would not return.

Farmisht was a good dog and the neighbors liked him, so they would bring him small bits of food, but he would not eat. He would not leave the front steps except to get a drink of water. He got weaker as time passed and, even though it was not winter, he would often shake with weakness and cold. But no matter what, he would do his job and wait.

When the war ended and the Jews were freed, Joel's mother went back to the family home in the hamlet. She wanted to know what happened to Farmisht. The neighbors told her that after Grandfather and his family were taken to the ghetto, Farmisht remained on the front steps of the home. The neighbors tried to feed him, but he refused food and died.

We were fortunate to survive. I moved to America, and Joel moved to Haifa, Israel. Even though Farmisht and Blackie were dogs, and this was a long time ago, we still feel their loss. They were part of the family.

Ketzelah

by Gloria Rubin

We had a beautiful female cat that helped to keep the mice from taking over our house. One day I opened my closet and could not believe what I saw.

"Mama, Mama, come quickly!" I called.

My mother came and looked in my closet and exclaimed, "Oh my, what have we here?"

To our surprise, our female cat had gone into my closet, pulled down my new dress, and produced a litter of kittens on my dress!

"Mama, look at my new dress! What will we do?"

"Don't worry," Mother told me. "We can wash and mend your dress."

My mother examined the newborn kittens and then took an old wooden box, filled it with rags and made a new bed for our cat. The cat gave Mother a contented look and settled into her new nest, where she then kept her kittens comfortable and warm.

As the kittens grew and their eyes opened, we noticed that one of the kittens was born with only one eye. She was a beautiful grey and white baby. My mother was partial to that kitten, so we kept her (in a day when deformed animals were usually killed), and called her Ketzelah.

The litter of kittens were funny to watch as they scampered around, pounced on shadows, chased each other, then fell asleep in one big pile. When the kittens were old enough, we found homes for all but the one-eyed kitten.

Ours was a busy household because my parents were kind, generous people who took in girls from an orphanage in our city—Nasielsk, Poland—and let them live with us until they got married and moved away. For me it was like having a huge family with many sisters.

Ketzelah viewed all of the people who lived in our home as "her" family. She always showed affection to anyone who let her curl up in their lap, or even sneak up onto a bed at night to burrow in the covers. She was a favorite companion to all of the girls and to us. Sometimes she would curl up on my lap and purr herself to sleep. I loved when she did that. Her contented look and gentle purring made me feel very special and happy. Maybe she was grateful that we gave her a home even though she only had one eye.

My father had a mill in Gawlova where he would grind wheat for the farmers.

A good mouser, Ketzelah helped keep the rodents under control at the mill. Often she would follow my father there, her tail straight up in the air with a little bend at the tip. She had a way of almost prancing when she walked, a light, happy gait. Sometimes if my father walked too fast for her, she would seem to call to him with a gentle little meow. "Slow down, wait for me!" Ketzelah was a very talkative cat.

My father always had a smile for people who brought their wheat to the mill and if Ketzelah was there, she would greet people with her cat smile. If she especially liked someone, she would rub against their leg and purr. The people who came to our mill always felt welcomed and would linger to chat. It was a pleasant, friendly time for us.

Once in awhile on warm days, I would find a quiet spot outside and sit with Ketzelah. I remember how sweet the air smelled and how warm the sun was. I would lean back with her on my lap dreaming about what I would be when I grew up. I would tell Ketzelah my plans and dreams, and she would look at me and then half close her eye and "smile" slowly, blinking at me. This was her contented look. Sometimes I would simply enjoy the time alone with her. With six brothers and sisters, as well as orphans in our house, solitude was a precious thing.

But the one who loved Ketzelah most was my mother. Often she would talk to Ketzelah as the cat followed my mother through the house while she worked in the kitchen or cleaned. When it got cold outside, Ketzelah would lie with her feet tucked under her body by the warm stove where my mother cooked. Mother kept an old rag folded into a bed near the stove for her.

Ketzelah was an unusual "people cat." Her behavior was more like a devoted dog. There seemed to be an understanding between my mother and Ketzelah; all of us saw it and admired their special relationship.

Then, in 1939, our world was torn apart. German soldiers came and forced all Jews to leave their homes and stand in the street. When this happened my father was not home and we were all afraid of what might have happened to him or where he could be.

My mother checked to see that all of us were together. We had heard horrible stories about being sent to camps. My mother remembered that Ketzelah was in the house and was afraid that the cat would die without food. Even though she was afraid of being shot or beaten, she begged the SS trooper to allow her to go back to the house and let Ketzelah out.

The SS trooper let her go back. My mother went into the house and found Ketzelah next to the still-warm stove. She picked her up, carried her outside and turned her loose. Mother was crying. "Try to understand," she told Ketzelah. "This is so you can live."

We were herded into cattle cars on the train to Lublin and then had to walk to the Warsaw ghetto, which took five days. Once we reached Warsaw, all of us—my mother, grandfather and seven of us children (I was the fifth) —lived in a room in the synagogue. My father was not with us; he was still free and trying to create an underground railroad for people to escape.

Food became hard to get and people would stand on the street calling for bread. We all stood on different streets begging for bread, sometimes taking turns. And faithfully each day my grandfather would stand on the street begging for food. Then one day he did not come back.

As it got late in the day, we became frightened about what could have happened to him. We did not want to think the unthinkable. Each of us went outside and searched the ghetto for him. We looked for him on each street, calling his name. Finally, after we looked as much as we dared, we returned back to our room. I remember how we all huddled together and cried, fearful of what may have happened to Grandfather. We knew that people sometimes disappeared from the ghetto.

The next day we gathered the courage to ask an SS trooper if they had seen Grandfather. Later that day there was a knock on our door and there stood an SS trooper. He was cold and hard. He told us that the soldiers had taken Grandfather away and that he had died the next day.

The SS troopers gathered the dead in one big hall

and had them buried in a mass grave in a cemetery on Gnsia St. The Germans let us go to the funeral. It was a horrible sight; people were distraught, crying and wailing. I felt so numb, thinking of my poor grandfather, a man I loved with all my heart being thrown into the mass grave. This was all unthinkable to a young child, these horrors that nobody should have to see or experience.

Life had to go on, and each day the younger children sat in the streets begging for food. I was one of those children. One day we were allowed to go from house to house to beg for food and I got some, but I was so hungry that I ate it. Immediately I felt so terrible about what I had done that I could not go home. The next day I did get some more food and I put it in a can and took it home. Mother sat all of the children down on the floor and gave each child one tablespoon of food.

We got so hungry that I said to my six-year-old brother, Sta, "Do you want bread?"

He said yes, so we formulated a plan to escape from the ghetto. We told my mother what we planned to do and, since so many people were "disappearing" and dying, she agreed.

The next day we pretended to beg for food as we made our way to the Polish side of the ghetto. Then we both escaped to the Polish side, outside the ghetto. We walked to a village ten miles away, where the Christian people knew us from the mill. We went from farm to farm begging them to hide us. We told them how people were starving and dying. We told them how we believed that Grandfather had been killed, and that we had seen his body dumped into a mass grave.

Finally, one farmer's wife let both of us stay. She said we could sleep in the stable with the animals. For us, this was heaven. We were warm and we felt safe.

Feeling safe and secure was short lived because, when my brother walked through the gate to the cow pasture to get bread, the cows ran from him, went into the cornfield and started to eat the corn. The farmer got mad and beat my brother. Every drop of food was important, and the farmer could not have the cows eating his corn.

At first we thought it would be easy to hide, but hiding turned out to be very stressful, and I got sick. We did not have the support of our family and could not be seen walking around the farm. We could not stay in the farmhouse either. I missed my family and found it hard to have to fend for myself and take care of my brother as well.

I was only thirteen years old and this life was difficult for a child who had always had a wonderful, safe life. As much as I was afraid of the ghetto, I missed my family. I felt alone and very afraid; but I knew if I went back to my family I would be caught and maybe shot. All I could think about was the

happy times when we were all together at home . . .
the times I sat with Ketzelah and felt her purring
contentedly . . . how she would blink her eye at me,
her way of saying, "I love you" . . . of summers in the
warm sun . . . of the fragrant smells of my mother's
cooking. I was so homesick that it hurt!

Every Friday was market day. The farmer's wife
had a booth to sell produce. Because I was not well,
she let me come with her one time. The market
was near our house, and the desire to see my home
overwhelmed me. I could not help how I felt. I wanted
to see where we had been happy. I felt that if I saw
my home I would get some sense of hope and peace,
the warm feeling of home. Then maybe I would feel
better.

I told the farmer's wife what I wanted to do and
she forbade me to go to our home. She was afraid
that someone would recognize me and turn her in to
the SS for hiding a Jew. That would mean that she
would be sent to the camps or shot.

However, while the farmer's wife was busy, I
quietly slipped away and walked to our home. I kept
my head down and wore a kerchief (scarf) to hide my
face. As I got closer to my home, I saw something on
our steps. I could not make out what it was at first.
But then I saw—it was Ketzelah! Alive! Joy flooded
my heart. How I longed to hold her and keep her with
me. Ketzelah saw me and recognized me right away,
and she cried as she ran to me.

Immediately I realized that anyone who knew our family and saw Ketzelah running to me would know it was me. Cold, hard fear gripped my heart and I turned to run away, but Ketzelah followed, crying to me. Finally, afraid that someone would see, I picked her up and hid her in my kerchief, taking her back to the market.

By this time it was late and few people were left at the market. When the farmer's wife saw Ketzelah, she knew what I had done. Her face became red and her eyes hard. She was terrified that someone would know that she was hiding me. She took a stick and beat me with it. I held Ketzelah in my arms, trying to protect her from the blows. However, the farmer's wife was angry at the cat and beat her too, breaking all of her legs and making her bleed.

Ketzelah cried in my arms, and I was crying uncontrollably. My tears fell on her little body. Out of fear, the farmer's wife beat us unmercifully. When she finally stopped, Ketzelah was bleeding and quiet.

"You go to the Christian cemetery and hide with that cat and wait for me. I will bring the horses and get you. But you will leave that cat in the cemetery!"

I was horrified and frightened beyond anything I had experienced before. I did not know if she was going to turn me in or help me.

I could not stop crying as I walked to the cemetery. My heart was broken, my beloved Ketzelah was hurt, and fear gripped me. Ketzelah was very quiet, barely making any noise. I held her, unable to put her down. My heart was breaking; she was my family, and she loved me. But, miracle of miracles, she was purring as she looked into my face. *Oh, what have I done?* I thought. How my mother's heart would be broken!

I sobbed, "Oh Ketzelah, my dear friend, I am so sorry. Please forgive me. I do not want to do this."

I saw the farmer's wife coming so I gently kissed her on the head and told her again how sorry I was, and then I laid her down behind a tombstone. I put my kerchief over her little body to try and keep her warm.

When the farmer's wife came near she told me, "I am taking you back home, and then you must leave."

I did not say a word all the way back to the farm. I did not know what to say. I was torn between love for my dear Ketzelah and fear of what would become of me and my brother. I couldn't hide the sobs that grabbed me from time to time.

The farmer's wife had a stony look on her face and would not look at me. Now I realize that she too was probably torn between her desire to help and her fear of the soldiers. Even after I left, if they found out she had helped me, they would take her away. Maybe even shoot her.

When I got back to the farm I found my little brother and took him into my arms, the tears streaming down my cheeks. "Sta," I said, "I couldn't help it. I went back to our house to look. I wanted to be home again. But there on the steps was Ketzelah. She ran to me and started to cry. I was afraid people would recognize me, so I picked her up and ran back to the market. The farmer's wife saw what I did and she beat me and Ketzelah. Sta, she broke all of Ketzelah's little legs. I left her in the Christian cemetery. I have to leave the farm."

Sta's eyes filled with tears and he grabbed me around my waist.

"Please don't go. Don't leave me," he begged through his tears.

"Sta, you can take care of yourself. You will be fine. Stay quiet and do not let anyone see you. I promise I will come get you when I find a safe place for both of us. I will stay in touch. Be strong."

We said good-bye, cried, and promised to stay in touch. Then I started my long walk to Novemiasto, another ghetto, about ten miles away. I was weak and it was an effort to place one foot in front of the other. I only had a little bread to eat and had to find water where I could. I think I had a fever because I felt hot and had chills. All I wanted to do was lie down and sleep, but I knew that it could mean death for me. My lips were parched and I only had the clothes on my back, which were not very warm. I had lost so much weight that my clothes hung loose on me.

When I finally arrived, the Jewish ghetto police

let me find a place to sleep under some steps. When I woke up, I managed to beg for some paper and I wrote to my mother and told her where my brother and I were staying. My mother rushed to my father, who was living on another street in their ghetto, and joyously told them where Sta and I were living. They had not known for sure what had happened to us.

As soon as they could, my father and mother left the ghetto and went to my brother and told him to wait until they found me, that they would come back for him. Next they walked to Novemiasto to find me.

When they found me they managed to get a room in a cellar for us to live. But things were getting worse for Jews. The soldiers had taken my older brothers and sisters to Auschwitz. So when my father returned to my brother, he told my brother to stay at the farm, because the Germans were taking people to Auschwitz and they had already taken my older brothers and sisters.

"Papa," cried Sta, "I want to go with you. Don't leave me here," he begged. But my father explained to him that the only reason we were not taken was because we had jobs cleaning the streets. Since there was no job for Sta, he was safer on the farm.

My father left my brother at the farm and returned to the ghetto, but Sta was a stubborn boy at times and he could not tolerate being away from Papa any longer. Sta cried for a few days, not able to bear the loneliness. Then Sta left the farm and walked for two days to reach my family. When he arrived at the ghetto, the Jewish ghetto police would not let him in. Sta cried from the bottom of his heart. He would not be comforted. He stayed at the ghetto gates and cried so much that they brought him to the cellar where we were staying.

On November 11, there was a commotion in the street. Papa told Sta and me to go into a corner and not to make a sound. I was so afraid, it was all I could do to not make noise, holding my sobs down deep inside me. Sta refused to leave my father and grabbed onto him and would not let go. Before Papa could do more, the door to our little room slammed open. The Germans grabbed my mother and father and shoved them into the street with many other people. The Germans tried to push Sta back into the room, they did not want him, but my brother cried and clung to Father. My father was crying, telling my brother and me to save ourselves, but Sta continued to cry and make such a fuss that the Germans took him, too.

I was the only one in my family to survive. Although I got married and adopted two lovely children and have owned dogs, cats and chickens, I still have a special place in my heart for our one-eyed, gray-and-white Ketzelah. She was a part of my family, she was a part of my mother. She represented the happier times of my childhood. She gave us love. The memories remain as vivid today as then.

3. BELGIUM

Although Belgium surrendered to the Germans on May 28, 1940, a mere eighteen days after being attacked, Belgium was the site of some famous battles of WWII. The Battle of the Bulge (Battle of Ardennes), which started on December 16, 1944, is considered the bloodiest battle of World War II with 19,000 American soldiers killed. The Germans planned to split the allied forces in half then circle round and destroy both halves independently. Then in the battle of Bastogne, General Anthony McAuliffe, although surrounded by the German army, refused to surrender. His famous response to the offer of surrender was to say, "Aw, nuts!" His official response to the Germans was simply, "NUTS!"

Despite the efforts of the Allies, July '42 saw mass deportations of Belgian Jews to concentration camps.

Unfortunately, Belgium has a history of anti-Semitism dating back to 1925 when the Jeunesse Nationale youth group was formed with the purpose of attacking Jews, Communists, Catholics and Freemasons.

Immediately after the Germans occupied Belgium in 1940, they instituted anti-Semitic laws banning Belgian Jews from certain professions, stole their property and businesses, and forced them into slave labor.

Many of the Jews who lived in Belgium had immigrated there after WWI. The Germans rounded them up and sent them to Breendonk and Mechelen, collection camps for the people who were to be sent to Auschwitz. Of the 25,000 who were deported to Auschwitz extermination camps, less than 2,000 survived.

Many non-Jewish citizens of Belgium hid Jews and it is estimated that they saved 25,000 from the camps.

The Cat

by Jacob Stern

Life in Belgium was not bad when I was a child. We had a nice house and a loving family consisting of my parents, a brother, a sister and myself. We also had a very funny cat. This cat loved to play and would chase a string and entertain us for hours at a time. I especially enjoyed it when the cat would sit next to me as I read a book. He would slowly close his eyes and blink—his way of letting us know he was happy and contented. Each member of the family had a unique relationship with him.

But World War II changed our lives drastically. There were families that would disappear, or the father of a family would not return. There were rumors that Jews were being sent to camps to do work or, as we suspected, to be killed.

The tension was mounting as more and more people were taken. Then one day the Germans told my father that he was to report to "work" in Germany.

My father gathered our family together and told us, "I want each of you to gather a small suitcase of clothes. We are going to hide in Brussels to get away from the Germans."

This was because my father suspected that his work assignment in Germany was not real and that he and all of us would be sent to the camps and killed.

We had to do this very quickly and not look obvious. So we were forced to leave everything except a few personal items.

As we were getting ready to leave I asked my father, "What about our cat? We cannot leave him behind."

Father said, "We have to look as casual as possible so that we do not cause suspicion. We must look like we are just going to visit relatives. We cannot take the cat."

I understood the need to look like a family on a casual outing. But the most heart wrenching of this episode was that we had to leave our beloved cat.

All of us cried because we were afraid for the cat, but my father promised that once we were all safe, he would send a truck back in a few days for some more of our stuff, including the cat.

A few days later we learned that, when the truck arrived at our house, the Gestapo had already discovered that we ran into hiding and sealed our house. Our neighbors told us that the Germans had loaded everything into two trucks and taken it away.

We never found out what happened to our cat. All

these years I have hoped that he escaped while the Germans were loading our stuff into the trucks and that someone adopted him.

Fortunately, all of my family survived. But we never forgot our cat.

4. HOLLAND

In many ways Holland suffered from the 1929 stock market crash; but most importantly for that time, the crash deeply cut into the Defense budget. This was one reason Holland was so ill prepared for World War II. Though Holland increased its Defense budget as the war in Europe progressed, they did not mobilize their forces until France and Great Britain declared war in 1939. Even then, Holland declared itself a neutral country, as it had done in World War I. The Dutch people did not anticipate going to war.

In the winter of 1939-1940 there were false alarms about the German invasion of Holland, so by the time Germany really invaded, the Dutch thought the warnings were false alarms, and ignored them.

When the German army attacked Holland, they faced only weak resistance from the Dutch forces, who were using weapons manufactured prior to 1900. The Germans out-gunned them.

After Germany captured Holland, the Dutch people and leaders expected the Allies to liberate them quickly, but because of the way the war progressed, this did not happen.

Adding to the situation, most of the Dutch public and the Dutch Jews did not believe that the Germans would practice genocide and send people to death camps. Furthermore, the openness of the Dutch landscape and the dense population made it difficult to hide Jews or operate a resistance. Therefore, the Germans were able to find and then kill one third of all the people who hid

Jews. *If any person supported the resistance or resisted the Germans, it meant being sent to the concentration camps or, possibly, instant death.*

Germany invaded the Netherlands on May 10, 1940. The Germans used the Dutch as forced labor, and although it was difficult, many Dutch people resisted the Germans by working poorly or very slowly. A Dutch family risked death if they hid Jews or helped downed Allies.

Nevertheless, many did do this as portrayed in the Diary of Anne Frank *and in* The Hiding Place *by Corrie ten Boom. The people who participated in the underground resistance movement were called* onderduikers. *Collectively they produced forged ration cards, counterfeit money, gathered intelligence, published newspapers, sabotaged phone lines and railways, prepared maps and distributed food and goods.*

With the invasion of Normandy, June 1944, the Allies moved quickly toward Holland. Even though parts of Holland were liberated in 1944-45, areas in the southern part of the country were not. The winter of 1944-45 was very severe and became known as the Hongerwinter *or Hunger Winter. Exhaustion, cold, disease and starvation claimed about 30,000 lives. Food was even scarcer because the Dutch government orchestrated a railway strike to try to force the defeat of the German army that still occupied Holland.*

Of the 140,000 Jewish people who lived in Holland at that time, only 30,000 survived the war.

Hanni

by Kurt Moses

My childhood in Germany was a rare one of peace and joy. I had parents who never fought or argued. My older sister, Lore (by three years) loved having a younger brother and doted on me. When I was born, we lived in Linnich, Germany where my father owned a small department store. I thought life in our small community was wonderful. People were friendly and I had many other children to play with. There was a strong sense of community. However, I was not aware that the seeds of hate had started to grow even there.

As the depression worsened, Jews were picked on and blamed for the economic problems in Germany. Neighbor turned on neighbor; people started to boycott the stores and businesses owned by Jews. Life became very difficult. Although my parents tried to shield my sister and me from the political situation and the fear that many Jews felt, we could still sense that things were not right.

By 1933 the political climate became bad enough for Jews that my father moved us to Sittard, Holland. He relocated his department store there. My parents couldn't understand the politically-motivated anti-

Semitic feelings toward Jewish people, and they believed that it would quickly pass. We would stay in Sittard until non-Jewish people came to their senses and the hatred passed.

I remember the night my father told my mother that we would move, and my mother expressed her perplexity. "Albert," she said to my father, "I have been friends with Greta for many years. She knows us; she knows our children who played with her children. How could she hate us?" Tears came to her eyes as she said, "She called me a nasty name and spat at me! We used to have lunch together and share recipes."

Life in Sittard settled down and we lived in relative peace. Of course news of the war came daily, but we believed that we would be safe in Holland. After all, Holland was a neutral country and did not want to be part of the war. However, it frightened me to know that people were fighting all around us.

One day in 1935 my father came home and made an exciting announcement.

"I have decided that we will get a German shepherd puppy." He said it very casually, but my sister and I clapped our hands and jumped for joy.

"When can we get him? When can we get him?" we asked, expecting to walk outside and he would be there.

When Father served in World War I, he had made friends with a man who bred and trained working German shepherd dogs of the best quality that Germany had to offer. This is where he would get our new puppy, he said.

My father made arrangements for his friend to meet us at the border of Holland to bring us our new six-month-old puppy. We dared not go into Germany.

I was about ten years old, at the time, and so excited. I will never forget the first time I laid eyes on Hanni von Rapttenbach, the most beautiful dog I had ever seen. He was descended from royalty and acted like it. Instead of wiggling or being anxious, he stood there calmly while my father paid the customs duty on him. He was regal, poised and already he was breathtakingly big.

From the moment we welcomed Hanni into our family, he was special to us. He was always a gentleman, always well behaved, and he made us feel safe.

My parents' bedroom was a few steps down from my sister's bedroom and my bedroom. Between the two levels was a small landing where Hanni slept through the night. This way he could watch over the whole family. We slept peacefully, knowing that he was always on guard.

Every night before my sister and I would go to bed, we had to lie down with Hanni on the landing and tell him a story. He would not settle down unless we performed this evening ritual. I often felt that he understood every word we said. Sometimes we would read to him, other times we would tell him about our day or make up a special story for him.

If the story wasn't all about him, we'd be sure to make him a part of the story. I think we comforted ourselves and eased our fears by making up stories about how Hanni saved us from one peril after another.

Alas, the hatred toward Jews found its way into Holland. I could not understand this, since the same children I had played with before, now did not want to be seen with me.

Years later I understood that some of it was because their fearful parents told them to stay away from us. There were rumors that German spies watched to see who was friendly to Jews. But at the time, I felt it was me personally that they did not like, and it hurt. As the situation for Jews continued to deteriorate, many of my friends no longer wanted to include me in their activities. Having Hanni as a friend and companion eased the rejection that I felt when boys my own age shunned me.

Hanni would often go for walks with my family and me; he was always ready to protect us. His presence in my life made me feel safe. His love for me was unconditional. Nevertheless, as much as my parents tried to protect my sister and me from the war, it finally came to our doorstep.

On May 10, 1940, at six o'clock in the morning my family was awakened by the loud sound of planes. We quickly got up and dressed, not knowing for sure what was happening. Everyone suspected that

Germany would try to invade Holland, but we could not be sure when. Then the rumor was that the invasion would be by land. Planes flew over Holland, but often they were allied planes going to or from someplace else. On that morning, however, low-flying German planes awoke us from sleep.

This was the start of the German invasion of The Netherlands. Holland had expected an attack by land and planned to flood the land to stop the Germans, but the Germans attacked by air. This quickly defeated any resistance or defense that the Dutch army had planned. We were helpless and all we could do was watch as the German troops marched into Holland. Hanni, sensing our fear, was ever watchful, staying by our side.

As soon as my father realized what was happening, that it was the invasion, he had us pack as many of our clothes as we could and some other possessions, and we all went to my mother's parents' home five miles away in Geleen. In this small town my father had his store. Mother's brothers and sisters also lived there.

Because Jews were not allowed to use motor vehicles, we had to pack what we could load and carry, onto bicycles. As soon as we were packed, we rode our bicycles to my grandparents' house. My parents rode a bicycle built for two while my sister Lore and I rode our individual bicycles. Hanni ran alongside as we pedaled to our relatives.

We tried to look as normal as we could, a family on an outing, and we did indeed look that way. However, inside we were very upset and deeply depressed. Hanni must have sensed this, since he stayed close to us. He usually ran ahead, loving visits to my grandparents' house for many reasons.

One reason was that my mother would cook a special meal for him of meat and rice, a nice change from his usual dog food. I always felt that Hanni loved my mother the best because she would make his special dinner. He was a very smart dog and knew that my mother cooked for him.

Everyone felt better being together and we prayed a lot. Finally, after things seemed to settle down and no German soldiers came looking for us, we went back to our home.

During the next two years, we would often visit my grandparents' home. But May 10, 1940 had been a turning point; and things only got worse from then on. We faced tighter food rations and spent many nights in an air raid shelter. The "Jew Laws" took over much of our lives, yet like many Dutch people, my parents felt that it would all pass quickly. They could not believe that people would continue with the madness.

However, as things turned out, November 11, 1942 was the worst, darkest day of our lives. At about one o'clock in the morning, there was a thunderous banging on our door. Everyone in the house panicked as my father went to answer the door.

There stood German soldiers.

"You have ten minutes to get dressed and pack! If you do not do what you are told we will shoot you," the soldier in charge barked at us.

They did not give us privacy to get dressed since they were afraid we would try to run or maybe had a gun in the house. We were shoved into the street, to be marched to the train station, half an hour away. Many others were already lined up on the street.

My father went to the German soldier in charge, even though he knew that he could be shot on the spot. "Please, sir, can our dog Hanni follow us so that we can leave him with the commissioner of police?" Hanni was standing right there, looking the German soldier in the eyes. Not nasty, but with a strong presence. The German looked at Hanni and hesitated for a moment.

"Yes," he said. "Your dog can follow. But if he tries to bite anyone, I will shoot him."

Once we reached Sittard's commissioner of police, a friend of my father's, he quickly knocked on the door and put Hanni inside. The commissioner knew what was happening, although he was helpless to do anything about it, and took Hanni, promising to take care of him.

As I saw my father order Hanni into the house, I could not help myself; I ran to our dog and hugged him around the neck. Crying, I promised him we would come back. My sister was by my side. She was crying. The police commissioner held Hanni by his collar in the doorway as we walked away. I thought I heard Hanni whine or give a low howl.

The blood of generations of champion working dogs ran through Hanni's veins. He had presence, the kind of presence that both humans and animals saw immediately. Hanni was never aggressive or mean; instead he sized up situations and decided what to do. If a stranger approached his family he would regard them until he was sure that they meant no harm, and then he was as friendly as any other dog.

Hanni's whole life was focused on protecting his family and being obedient. Like many generations of his noble breed, his devotion was unfailing.

When his family was herded into the street, he knew that they were afraid. He knew that most of the people were afraid; he could hear fear and smell fear. He knew that the men with rifles were a threat; but he was told to leave them alone.

When the German soldier looked at him as he talked to the father, he stared back, unfaltering, unwavering, and the man backed down because he felt Hanni's "presence."

When the father put him into a strange house, his instincts screamed that he should stay on guard with his family, but his obedience also came into play when he was told to stay.

Long after things quieted down, Hanni struggled,

torn between his desire to be with and protect his family and his desire to be obedient to the command to stay.

Weeks passed and his family did not return. Hanni became increasing stressed, and then depressed. Finally he knew what he had to do, where he had to be . . .

We had only a moment to say our good-byes to Hanni as we were pushed along to the train station. We felt relieved a tiny bit that my father had talked to the police commissioner before this happened and had made arrangements that if we were deported, he would take care of Hanni. That was like my father; he took good care of all of us, always thinking of our safety and happiness.

We felt that at least one family member would be safe. The sight of Hanni standing next to the commissioner by his front door, as I waved good-bye to my friend and companion, is etched into my mind, even now.

We were loaded onto trains that were already crowded with people from previous stops, but we were together still.

Westerbork, a camp located in the northeastern town of Drente, Holland was our first stop. We were ordered to register and turn over all of our possessions for "safe keeping." Then we were given numbers on cards hanging from our necks, assigning us to different barracks.

I had never felt so afraid. I was just seventeen, without contact with my family and forced to live in a barracks with hundreds of other men, all strangers to me. I did not know who I could trust or who I couldn't. Not everyone was friendly, and some people would try to steal what they could from you. Food and clothes were scarce. The Germans made us give up anything we had, that they needed or wanted. I was not so strong that I could defend myself from everyone.

I got sick with diphtheria and spent several weeks in Westerbork's large hospital. We were led to think that the Germans wanted people healthy so that they would be a good work force. But often people who got sick and recovered were shipped out on another train. We assumed it was to a labor camp but we never knew for sure. Every Tuesday morning, about a thousand people were shipped out on the train that had arrived the night before.

One day the Germans ordered us to prepare to leave. It was a good day for me because I learned that my mother, father and sister were leaving on the same train. The Germans sent all of us to Theresien-stadt in Czechoslovakia. The joy of it was that I was able to see my family again and I could stay with my father. We were there for a while, then my father and I were loaded onto another train to be sent to yet another camp. We had no idea where. It was very hard to leave my mother and sister, but we were hopeful that we would be reunited soon.

My father and I managed to stay together while we were on the train and even after we arrived at Auschwitz. The SS forced us to leave what little belongings we had at the train station, marched us five abreast and beat us with sticks.

We were marched in front of a German officer who had a calm air of detachment. As each prisoner marched before him, he would point with his raised cane, right or left, indicating where the person should go. It was my turn; the cane pointed right. Next came my father, and the cane pointed left. While I was not happy, I was not too worried; it only seemed natural that my father and I would go to different work units. I was sure we would both survive and be reunited.

I later learned that the man with the cane was the infamous Dr. Mengele. All of the men that he sent to the left went straight to the gas chambers. I never saw my father again.

By the grace of God, I survived Auschwitz. My talent in woodworking kept me alive because I was useful to the Germans. A Polish woman, who worked at the camp, risked her life to sneak food to me. As Germany fell, a few friends and I managed to hide from the Germans, who were forcing the prisoners on a last march. We escaped Auschwitz. We roamed the countryside and found food, shelter and clean clothes. We were able to bathe, a luxury that we had not had for a while.

As soon as possible, my friend Leo and I went back to Auschwitz. That was the last place I had seen my father; I hoped that I might find him still alive. When I learned that he had not survived, I headed for Theresienstadt where I had last seen my mother and sister. With much effort, I did find them still in the area, alive.

We were able to return to Sittard, our home in Holland, and I was able to find work. All this time, Hanni remained foremost in my mind. He was part of my father, part of my family. At the very first chance, my sister Lore and I went to the police commissioner's house. We were both feeling hopeful, fairly sure that Hanni would have survived the war as we had.

We knocked on the commissioner's door, but did not hear a dog bark. There wasn't a German shepherd in sight. Maybe, I hoped, Hanni was playing somewhere, and would return shortly. The commissioner answered the door and I could see a shadow cross his face. He invited us into his parlor and, after we sat down, told us what had happened.

"After your family left, Hanni refused to eat. He would run away and go to your house, where he sat on the front stoop—tall, looking, waiting. I could see that he was watching and hoping to spot you and your family coming home. I would bring him back here and try to get him to eat, but he refused food.

One day he ran away again. I went to your home
and saw him lying with his back pressed against your
front door. When I called, he did not move, and I
realized that he had died. I think he died of a broken
heart."

As the commissioner told us what had happened
to Hanni, my sister Lore started to sob. As I took
Lore out of the commissioner's house, he stopped me
long enough to press something into my hand. It was
Hanni's collar. I shook the man's hand and thanked
him for doing what he could for Hanni.

I always felt that Hanni could have survived; he
was only seven or eight and in perfect health when
we left him. World War II has forever torn my family
apart. Some of us survived, others did not. Although
the loss of my father and other relatives is something
that I never fully recovered from, Hanni was also part
of our family, and I never fully recovered from the
loss of my beloved and faithful dog.

Brady

by Joyce Clemens

Hans, my mother's ex-husband, was one of the select few who were allowed to hunt in Holland because he had hunting dogs. Hans gave my mother a hunting spaniel named Brady. The Germans valued working animals and because Brady was a hunting dog, they allowed Hans to send a suitcase of kibble to my mother each week for Brady.

It was October 1944, the beginning of what the Dutch people called "The Hunger Winter." At that time my mother was remarried to a man named Hendrik and we lived in the southern part of Holland.

I remember when Hendrik came rushing into the house, my mother and I could tell immediately that he was excited.

"We did it, Anna, we have a railway strike set for next week. It will mean that we will suffer from lack of food, but so will the Germans. It will help to defeat them."

"How will we survive?" my mother asked.

"Anna, dear Anna, our lives are not as important

as defeating the Germans. But we will survive."

Everyone who knew about the upcoming railroad strike started to gather and hoard whatever
food they could store. But one week was not enough
time to gather much, especially when there was so
little.

As the winter wore on, food became harder
to find. People ate anything, even tulip bulbs, to
stay alive. Nevertheless, Brady was fairly well fed,
because the Germans gave working animals food.

City animals and people suffered more than
those in the country because there was more food in
the country. For this reason Hans would often go to
the country to barter for food to send to us.

The people in the country were very kind and
were more than willing to share what they had
with the city dwellers, both animals and people. The
farmers from whom Hans got food had extra dogs
and cats on their farm because, when their neighbors and friends were taken by the Germans to the
ghetto, the farmers took in their pets to care for
them as best as they could. People were optimistic
that eventually the people taken away would come
back.

As the war continued, the time came when even
Hans could not send food for us or Brady. But we
were lucky to live in Rotterdam where there was
a milk factory at the end of our street. I would go
there every week to get some milk for Brady. The

Germans made the dairy workers account for every drop of milk because it was rationed for everybody. But, still, they would give us some for Brady.

Finally the time came when they could spare very little milk. The cows were starving and producing less. But the workers continued to take the risk, giving us some milk so that Brady could live. Even though we were hungry, we loved Brady so much, we would not drink his milk.

People started to starve. This is when they resorted to eating tulip bulbs. And then house pets were often stolen and eaten.

One day Hendrik sat us down and told us, "The van den Bergs have killed their cat and buried it in a secret place. They would not even tell me. Their poor little girl, Wimke, is inconsolable. She will not stop crying for the cat."

I felt so bad that the next day I went to visit Wimke and took Brady with me. Wimke hugged Brady for a long time, and even though Brady was weak, he let her hold him for as long as she wanted.

Between her sobs she asked me, "Do you think cats go to Heaven?"

"Yes," I told her, "I am sure that they do." I was not really sure, but I wanted to console her. She accepted what I said and asked God to give her cat a good home.

This incident was not unusual since many people decided that rather than risk having their pets caught and eaten, or eating their pets themselves, they would put the animal to sleep and bury it where no one would find the body.

I'll never forget one evening in January, 1945. Our family sat down for our one meager meal of the day. Hendrik had been able to catch two weak song birds, which we put into a stew pot with a few tulip bulbs and other things we could find, maybe some weeds or grass (but I did not want to know what they were).

We had not been able to get food for Brady for some time, and we could not get the little bit of milk for him like we used to. The cows were barely productive; people were starving.

Brady looked at us as we sat down to eat, but there was no food for him. We could not look at him. His ribs and hip bones stuck out and his eyes had a hollow look. Even though he was starving to death, he still loved us and would snuggle when he could.

Hendrik said a prayer before we started to eat. Then he quietly said, "I think it is time we put poor Brady out of his misery. He cannot last much longer, and we have no idea when the war will end. We cannot feed ourselves, let alone him."

No one said a word. Each of us had tears in our eyes. I slipped a small crust of bread into the pocket of my apron to give Brady later. I did not want him to die with nothing at all to eat.

We dearly loved Brady and he was a loyal

member of our family; but we all knew it was true. We had to protect Brady every day, keeping him near us when he was outside, walking him only at night when people would not see him. We had to guard him during the day because starving people might try to steal him from our house if he were home alone. We were so weak that we were not sure if we could fight off someone stronger who would want to take Brady. We did not want anyone to kill and eat Brady, and eating him ourselves, even though we were starving, was not an option.

Brady looked at us as though he understood. That night as Brady curled up next to me in bed trying to get warm, I slipped him the small crust of bread. As hungry as he was, he gently took it from my fingers. I looked into his eyes and I knew he appreciated my sacrifice for him. He could hear my empty stomach grumble as it did most of the time. I gave him a hug, trying not to cry and then fell into an exhausted sleep.

After everyone in the family had gone to bed and was fast asleep, Hendrik gently carried Brady outside and killed him. He took care to bury him in a deep hole which he hid so no one would find him. Even we did not know exactly where Brady was buried.

When I woke up that morning, I knew my beloved Brady was gone. I cried for myself, my family, and my innocent Brady.

We all gathered together and held a special memorial for Brady. Somehow it made us all feel a little better.

Looking back on it, even if we had known that the end of the war was just a few months away, Brady would not have survived. He was too far gone. I understand now how hard it must have been for Hendrik to do what he had to do, and how much he loved Brady to do it.

5. ROMANIA

In 1941 Romania declared itself as a neutral country not wanting to participate in World War II. Then, in June that year, Romania joined the Axis Powers.

Later, when Romania's dictatorship was overthrown, it joined the Allies (1944). Due to problems with Russia, though, the Greater Romania was not to survive after the war and lost territory to Bulgaria and the Soviet Union.

During the time that Romania was ruled by a pro-Nazi dictatorship, up to 380,000 Jewish people were murdered.

Besides being anti-Semitic with harsh laws against Jews (such as stripping them of their citizenship) the "Iron Guard" which ruled Romania also passed laws against Armenian and Greek businessmen. By October 8, 1940 there were over 500,000 Nazi troops in Romania.

Ion Antonescu ruled Romania from 1940 to 1944. He was responsible for forcing Jews to leave the countryside and move to urban centers. He stole Jewish property and businesses. He was responsible for the death of up to 380,000 Jews. Many of them died a slow death while being shipped on trains across the country. Many Jews were killed in pogroms, a Russian term for a violent riot or mob attack.

An example of these attacks are the Riga Ghetto Massacres, where civilian citizen nationalists arrested, beat, tortured and raped Jews while burning synagogues with people inside. They drove people to beaches or forests where they were shot to death. Those that survived were sent to the concentration camps to be killed.

Jannet, Marcela & Cheelly

by Lya Galperin

We lived in a *shtetle* (townlet) consisting mostly of Jews and Greeks. My father owned the mill and was an important man. We were well-to-do people and lived a good life.

Twice a week was a special time in our townlet. It was a time for business and socialization when the residents of smaller villages came to the farmers market in our larger village. They would do business with the shop owners and seek solutions to their problems.

During market time they would see lawyers, doctors, hairdressers, barbers, etc.—whatever business needed to be done. It was a social time as well; friends met and talked about everything under the sun. I loved these times, especially in the summer when I was not in school, when I could join in the fun.

For the most part, the Greeks ran the produce stores and restaurants. The Jewish people owned the bookstores, library, picture house, schools and of course, the synagogue. This made them the spearhead of the social life.

My father had a grain mill that was three stories high. He not only processed the grain, but handled everything related to grain. Because he was honest and kind, he was well respected and admired; most people knew him. This made my life exciting since everyone who knew my father, also knew me. Life was good and we were happy.

We had three mixed-breed terriers at the time. Our dogs were about the size of a spaniel, not big but not small either. All three of them were black and tan with a little bit of gray. Jannet was the mother and her two puppies, Marcela and Cheelly, were about eight months old. I loved my dogs and enjoyed playing with them every day. Sometimes I would throw something for them to chase. Marcela and Cheelly would make a mad dash for the object and sometimes Jannet would join in. Other times she would stay with me and look at her pups as if they were silly. But I always thought she had love in her eyes for them. These dogs fostered in me a lifelong love of dogs that has never lessened.

Often the dogs would try to follow us to the market. My father did not want them to follow us and get into mischief, so we would tell them to go home. They learned what this meant and would wander back home to wait for us, knowing that sometimes I would bring them a special treat from the butcher.

When the war started, my parents hid their fear from us children. But the fear permeated the townlet, so even though the adults did not talk about it, we kids could sense that something was not good. My parents, like many others, would talk quietly, out of earshot, but the tension and fear showed in their faces. Even Jannet, Marcela and Cheelly seemed to lose some of their joy of life. I noticed that they became quieter, and would often stay near us rather than wander like they used to do.

Even market days were not the same. People would talk quietly in small groups, with somber looks on their faces. Sadness and fear slowly descended on everyone, and little by little, people would not show up at the market.

Today it is hard for people to understand what it was like in those days. Some people had radios, but many of the stations were controlled by the Germans. There were only a few stations that told the truth, that were controlled by the allies.

We had newspapers but the stories could be old by the time the reporters received the information. Sometimes we had newsreels that were shown at the theater. Thus, information traveled slowly, unreliably and many times by word of mouth.

The children would compare notes, and we put together what we thought was happening—a bit heard from this conversation, a bit from that. We realized that some of the families who disappeared had fled the townlet. I was afraid to ask my parents if we were going to run away too. I worried about my friends who did not come to play anymore. Adults did not seem to realize that children have a way of piecing together what is going on. Sometimes our stories were grander than they should have been, and we became very frightened. It was during these times that the dogs would comfort us.

By May of 1941 we all knew about the war and feared the Nazis. My parents could not hide the war from us any longer.

Just after breakfast early in June 1941 my father rushed home from the mill. He had learned that the Romanian Nazis were advancing fast and were getting close. As hard as it was to leave his mill, my father had decided that we could not stay.

"I want everyone to gather a few things, clothes for the winter, even though it is not cold now. Children, you can take just one of your favorite things."

We rushed to gather a few items of clothing. Fearful and excited, we called to our mother about what we should take. The dogs were jumping and barking as we rushed around, running outside to load our suitcases into two small carts. Since we could only take the bare necessities, it didn't take us long to pack. With the dogs trotting along with us, we left our home.

As we hurried down the road, the dogs seemed to perk up a bit. My parents pushed us as fast as we could go; they were afraid that the Nazis would catch up to us. It seemed as though we could not travel as fast as my parents wanted; our small feet could not go faster. We got tired. Even now I wonder how my father and mother managed to push the carts as fast as they did. We all would help as best we could, our small hands next to their larger ones, pushing to help them go faster.

We traveled quite far, crossing two rivers. We could hear the trucks getting closer behind us. We could see the dust they were raising on the road behind us. Other people had joined us, trying to outrun the Nazis. Everyone became panicky.

Finally, we heard the harsh words we dreaded. "Halt! Halt now!" And we heard the click of the rifles. The Nazis had caught us. We had waited too long to leave.

The Nazis grabbed what they wanted from the carts, mostly valuables and food, which many people took with them. Then they forced us to strip off our clothes, looking for any valuables we may have hidden. The dogs stayed near us, fearful and unsure of what was going on. The Nazis ignored the dogs; and I was hopeful that after they took what they wanted, they would let us all go.

One soldier ordered all the people to take off their jewelry. My mother was so frightened and embarrassed that her hands were shaking.

"You! Get that ring off now!"

My mother struggled, but the ring had been on a long time and would not come off easily. Before I realized what was happening, the soldier slapped my mother across the face.

Without hesitation, to protect my mother, Jannet leapt through the air and attacked the soldier, grabbing him by the thigh and hanging on. The soldier stabbed Jannet with his bayonet, killing her instantly.

I gasped. Then I panicked and yelled at Marcela and Cheelly: "Go home! Run home! Run!"

Both dogs took off, but once or twice they stopped and looked back. My eyes met theirs, and I could see my own fear and uncertainty mirrored in their faces. It broke my heart and made me even more afraid, but I yelled again: "Go home!"

Once we were dressed again, our small group of people were herded into a ghetto. Life became a living nightmare. There was little or no food. People would stand or sit on the corners and beg for food. Some people in the ghetto, who had not been thoroughly searched and had sewn jewelry and money into the hems of their clothes, would try to barter for food. People died every day. Families were often separated by the Germans, taken to a place we did not know about.

We were lucky because we stayed together as a
family for three years, and we survived. Then one
day late in 1944 civilians came into the ghetto telling
the people that they represented a Jewish organization called JOINT.

These civilians gave hope to many of the families
in the ghetto. There was a glimmer of joy at the
message they brought. They claimed that they had
negotiated terms with the Nazis, that for money,
children up to fifteen years of age would be sent to
Palestine! The civilians explained that at first the
children would be sent to a nearby city and prepared
for the trip. Next they would be sent to the coastal
city of Constanta in Romania, and finally put on
ships to Palestine.

Our family talked about it as did many other
families. The outcome was that many parents
agreed to do this because they felt that there was
no hope for the children in the ghetto, that at least
the children would be taken care of, survive, and get
to Palestine.

I remember the day well. We all hugged, families
were torn apart, their children taken, but with hope
for a better life. We were starving in the ghetto;
and this was a chance to go to Palestine. It was
a very bittersweet day—one mixed with hope and
sadness—when they took us away.

The people marched us to the nearby city of
Balta. There they put us in a hospital where we were

bathed, given food and clean clothes, and placed in large rooms. We were to be checked by doctors before we could continue our trip. We ate warm, good food. We all felt better being fed, clean, and in a place that was nice compared to the ghetto. The room was full of hope and a measure of happiness.

Then the nightmare started. We were herded into a big room in the basement of the hospital. Though there were a number of rooms, we were kept in one. We had to sit, and even sleep, on the hard floor. A guard at the door made sure we did not leave. Then the nurses and doctors came in to draw blood from us.

The girl sitting next to me commented, "More blood!? How many tests must they do before we can go to Palestine?"

Then the nurses started coming more often for blood. We soon realized that we were not in the shelter of JOINT but were captives of the Germans, and that the Nazis were using us as blood donors. Word of this spread through the room. One larger boy who was still pretty strong, fought with the nurse when she tried to take blood from him. Immediately the guards came and beat him. The boy had no choice but to let the nurse take blood. He died shortly after, I think from being beaten and drained of so much blood. I think this is why the Nazis only wanted children fifteen years old and younger, so that they would not be strong enough to fight.

They need not have worried too much since most of the children were too weak to fight. The more blood the Nazis took, the weaker we got. Many of the children died or were too weak to give enough blood. I had been giving blood for a few months, and since I was type O, I was one of the children who were used a lot.

I became so weak that I slipped into a trance or sleep-like state. I did not feel as though I was there. I hallucinated: I saw my family; I thought I was holding Jannet, Marcela and Cheelly. I thought that I was home again. I felt warm, then cold. I thought I could smell my mother's dinner cooking.

Then in the spring of 1945, as a German nurse was taking my blood, I passed out. The nurse thought I was either dead or soon to be dead.

I remember feeling cold and dark, as if I were floating, being carried by my feet and arms. I had felt that way before. Then, there was nothing but darkness, but I was still vaguely aware of my surroundings. I slipped into a memory of my home and summer. . . .

My next sensation was of something round like a ball hitting me in the small of my back; I thought I felt either Marcela or Cheelly's fur rubbing against me. Then it felt like I was lying on branches, then darkness again. Next, quite suddenly, it got very warm and the sun was shining. I was sitting by the stream at home; Jannet, Marcela and Cheelly were playing nearby. We had a picnic spread on an old blanket and they came over to get a treat. Then darkness, cold, and the branches pushing on my body, above and below.

I don't know how long I lay there before I heard a deep Russian voice say, "This one's alive! Over here. Give me a hand."

Next, I again had the sensation of floating. Only this time I was on something soft, and warm food was put into my mouth. Slowly I regained consciousness.

I learned later what had happened: I became so weak from losing blood, that the Germans thought I was dead. I was put in another room in the basement on the pile of dead bodies, to be buried in a mass grave. I was so close to death that I hardly thought about it. It was like being in a dream. The fear and horror would creep in, pushing through the darkness, as though it was pushing through a cloud, and I was helpless to do anything about it. I did not think much; I was only aware of feelings, sensations.

The branches were the skinny legs and arms of the bodies of the other children, the round balls their heads and what I thought was the fur of my beloved dogs, their hair. I was buried alive in a pile of bodies.

Shortly after I was tossed on the pile of bodies, the Soviet Army came and liberated the city of Balta, but they withdrew. Then in a few days they came back and retook the city.

Children being used as blood donors was a well-kept secret. No one knew what was happening to us; even the local citizens did not know about the bodies in the basement, so the Russian soldiers had no idea that we were there.

As the soldiers searched the city, and finally the basement of the hospital, they found us in one of the rooms in the basement. I lay there in an unconscious and semiconscious state for a few days.

The children who were still alive were taken to a military hospital where they received medical care. When they recovered enough to travel, many of the children were sent to Soviet orphanages; but I was lucky. A medical aide recognized me because before the war he had married a neighbor's daughter from our village.

He was given a week to go to the ghetto to look for his family and in doing so, he found my mother; I was reunited with my family. What a glorious day that was. I had given up hope, not only of finding my family alive, but of getting home and finding Marcela and Cheelly.

After three and a half years of being separated from our home, my family slowly made our way back to the village and the mill. It was hard since we all suffered from ill health and lack of food. Many times while I lived in the ghetto I wondered about Marcela and Cheelly. Did they survive? Had someone taken them in and loved them like I did? I hoped that when we got home, someone would be able to tell us what had happened to them.

In my mind I could feel their soft fur as I hugged them around the neck and kissed their cute cheeks. I could feel their warm kisses as they licked my hands or my chin. I thought of the days when we ran in the stream next to the mill, chasing small fish or just relaxing in the sun, watching birds.

How warm and comfortable life was back then. How dark and cold it seemed now. *Will I ever be happy again? Will I ever feel good again? What does the future hold? Is there even a future?* These were big questions for a young girl.

Finally our house was in sight. The front door was opened; it was moving slightly with the breeze, and some of the windows looked broken. I guess I did not expect our house to be the same as when we left, but this was disappointing all the same. When I stepped inside, it was cold and dark. People had taken what they wanted from the things we left behind. People had searched for food to eat, clothing to keep them warm, and fuel for fires.

Almost upon entering the house, out of a dark corner there was a slight movement. Was it a rat or some wild creature? The skinny, dirty form came toward me and my breath stopped. "Cheelly?" I called.

Yes, it was my Cheelly, my dear, beloved Cheelly.

He had waited; he had survived all this time. He looked awful—skinny, dirty and wild—but I didn't care. He rushed to me, and I buried my face in his fur, crying. We both had survived; except for Jannet and Marcela, we all had survived. Life looked better; there was hope.

As soon as I could, I gave Cheelly a bath and shared my food with him. That night he slept in my bed with me, and I know that as I held him tightly, he felt the same joy I did. As he lay down next to me, he gave a long, deep sigh, almost as if he were saying, "Now I can sleep in peace again."

Although we never found out what happened to Marcela, Cheelly lived to be fourteen. For the rest of his life he hated military uniforms and boots. He was a very loving dog and very, very much loved by all of us. Although we were sad not to have Jannet and Marcela with us, we felt blessed to have Cheelly.

6. FRANCE

In 1939, after Germany invaded Poland, France and England declared war on Germany. This was the beginning of WWII. In 1939-40 France engaged in what was called "the Phony War": for six months, neither France nor England did anything. Then in January 1940 France enacted food rationing. England issued ration cards for butter, sugar, bacon and ham. On June 10 the Fascist government of Italy declared war on England and France. On June 14 the Sixth German Army entered Paris. June 22, on what was recorded as a beautiful French day—the kind that songs have been written about, France signed an armistice with Germany at Compiègne, the exact spot where France had signed a WWI armistice with Germany in 1918.

This armistice, in effect, made almost two-million French citizens prisoners of war. Then in December 1942 The Family Hostage Law was passed which said the "terrorist" families who did not surrender to Germans could expect the men in their families to be killed instantly, the women sent to work camps, and the children sent to schools for "political re-education."

Anti-Semitism, strong throughout France, was especially strong in Vichy France. The government at Vichy worked with the Germans to identify Jews for deportation to camps, and they passed anti-Jewish laws.

In 1942 alone, almost 76,000 Jews were sent to Drancy, the French holding camp, then to Nazi death camps. Most of the Jews deported were not French, however. Vichy did try to protect its native French Jews from deportation—ironically, France has the third highest number of Righteous Among the Nations awards (according to a Vashem Museum report in 2006) which were given by the state of Israel to non-Jews who risked their lives during the Holocaust to save the lives of Jews.

Nicolas

by Yvonne Rothschild Klug
(Yvonne Redgis)

I was a ballet instructor and lived with my non-Jewish husband in Cavalaire-sur-mer (near St. Tropez) on the French Riviera. The times were tense. In 1935 France became aware that Germany was preparing to occupy the Rhineland, the demilitarized zone. As citizens, we were not sure what would happen to us. But France as a whole did not want to engage in what would be considered an act of war by confronting the Germans. So without resistance, Hitler's army took over the Rhineland.

On Sunday, March 8, 1936 the headlines in the Paris newspaper, *Le Matin*, led everyone to believe that Hitler's move into the Rhineland was good for France and that the French people should be grateful because he saved them from the communists.[1]

---

1. The French did not know that Hitler was nervous about moving into the Rhineland and had ordered the German soldiers to beat a hasty retreat if they saw French troops. (*The Collapse of the Third Republic*, William L. Shirer, 1969, pg. 267)

The political climate in France from 1936 to 1940 was full of ups and downs. In 1936 there were strikes by workers in factories across the country. During this time Léon Blum became the President of France. It was the first time a Jewish person held this office. At this time, also, a strong wave of anti-Semitic feeling was directed at Léon Blum.

Many French people hated Blum with a passion. The anti-Semitic attitude made many of the French Jews nervous. It added to the continuing threat we felt from Hitler's hatred of the Jewish people.

The next few years were full of turmoil in France. There was political upheaval with news of Germany's advances and movements; still France did not want to engage in war. Life settled into a routine. The feeling prevailed that there was no need to suffer or deprive oneself of the good, easy life. Daily living returned to just about normal.

During November of 1939, the arts still flourished. Maurice Chevalier and Josephine Baker performed at the Casino de Paris. Lucienne Boyer was singing again at her boîte in the rue Volney. Henri Bernstein had a new play, *Elvire,* and in the theater there was a new Baty play, *Phèdre.* My ballet students continued their studies. Life was not so bad, even when France declared two meatless days per week. Everyone felt that this was acceptable, because they could have all they wanted on the other five days.

Within a few days of the armistice, by June

17, the Germans marched into Paris. The streets of
Paris were devoid of their usual teeming populace,
except for a few German soldiers strolling along
the walkways. Many French people had fled France,
especially those who suffered under the Germans in
World War I. My husband and I elected to stay, but
since the Armistice in 1940, I had been involved with
the French underground. I wanted to fight for my
country and home. For the most part I would spy on
the Germans to see what they were doing and where
they were going. It was very stressful but also in a
way, exciting. I was glad to do it because I was doing
my part for my beloved France.

About a year before the Armistice, realizing that
you have to take joy where you can find it, I had
decided to get a wonderful French bulldog puppy. I
had admired the breed for a long time and followed
the lines of the more famous of the French bulldogs.
Therefore I was familiar with the sire of the litter
and the lines. Little did I know at the time what an
adventure my dog and I would have over the next
few years.

After what seemed like forever, the puppies were
born—all eight of them. As the puppies grew, I
would go and watch them as often as I could. This
was a totally enjoyable few hours as I tried to decide
which one I wanted. I was lucky because the owner
of the puppies allowed me to have my pick of the
litter. Later, I would learn that my eye for beauty

and form would pay off; but I did not know it at the time.

I remember sitting for a very long time studying the litter, watching the puppies play and trying hard to pick "my" special friend. The puppies were six weeks old and all of them were so cute. Nothing is quite as relaxing and joyous as sitting down to play with a litter of puppies. They'd climb on my lap, playfully pull at my clothes, and nibble on my fingers. But one puppy seemed to want to stay with me the most. I chose this cute black-and-white puppy. Then, finally, the time came for me to pick up my Nicolas and proudly carry him home.

What a life he had, spoiled by someone who doted on him daily. I took seriously my job of raising and training him to be a model citizen of our town. I purchased a nice collar for him that included a nametag so if he ever ran away, whoever found him would return him to me. Later, this would prove to be one of the best things I did for Nicolas.

During the next year, I would take Nicolas on a daily walk, teaching him not to pull on the leash. He also had to learn to sit, to come when I called him, and not to beg for food.

He grew to be a fine young dog with a sleek coat, weighing about thirty pounds. I would always sneak him a bit of food from my plate. Despite my spoiling, he was a gentleman and a delight to have as my best friend.

The one thing I could never get him over, though, was his dislike of cats. Just like many bull-dogs, Nicolas hated cats. As far as I could tell, he never had a bad experience with them, but he would chase cats every chance he got.

When he was still young, we went on a vacation and, to my horror, I learned that the hotel had six resident cats, who had the run of the place.

The first time we went for a walk, one of the cats ran in front of Nicolas and he tried to sprint after it.

"No!" I said to Nicolas. "You must leave the cats alone. These are the cats that live here."

Each time Nicolas would try to chase a cat I had a serious talk with him and told him "No!" in a firm voice. I purposely walked him near the cats as often as I could the first few days so that he would learn the lesson quickly. And, after a few days, he seemed to understand that these cats were some-thing special and that he was not allowed to attack them. This, of course, took an immense effort on his part; but being a well-behaved dog, he obeyed me.

Things went smoothly for a while and then sud-denly I saw Nicolas chasing a poor cat. The cat barely made it up a tree to safety from Nicolas's deadly attack. I was horrified and went to the owner of the hotel to apologize.

He came out smiling and said, "This is alright,

MODÈLE DÉPOSÉ

PEDIGREE

Modèle de la Société Centrale Canine pour l'Amélioration des Races de Chiens en France

RECONNUE D'UTILITÉ PUBLIQUE

PARIS (2ᵉ) - 3, Rue de Choiseul - PARIS (2ᵉ)

Certificat de Naissance

Je soussigné *Jean Messelet*

Demeurant à *Paris 8 rue Huysmans*

Propriétaire de la lice *Kichanne*

Espèce *Bouledogue français* Née le *30 sept. 1936*

Robe *Bringée* L.O.F. Nº *9 B F 625*

dont pedigree ci-contre,

Certifie que saillie par le seul étalon *Laïus du*
travers junvet

Cette lice a mis bas le *15 avril 1939*

une portée de *quatre* chiots dont le produit :

Nom *Nicolas*

Sexe *Masculin* , Taille

Poids

Robe *Bringée*

Marques particulières

Fait à *Paris*
le *1 juin 1939*

Le propriétaire de la lice :

jean messelet

Propriétaires successifs :

Yvonne Redgis-Keup

Certificat de Saillie

M *René G. Lecomte*

demeurant à *Paris, 4 Rue Nevan 16*

Propriétaire de l'étalon *Laïus des travers* *junvet*

Espèce *Bouledogue français* Né le

Robe *Bringée* L.O.F. Nº *9 B F 502*

dont pedigree ci-contre,

Certifie que cet étalon a sailli les *10 et 13 février 1939*
la chienne *Kichanne*

Mère de *Nicolas*

faisant l'objet du présent pedigree.

Fait à *Paris*
le *14 Février 1939*

Le propriétaire de l'étalon *R. J. Lecomte*

Timbre de Contrôle
Société Centrale Canine
de France
3, Rue de Choiseul, Paris
LIVRE DES ORIGINES
Numéro d'inscription

L.O.F.: 9.B.F. 672

Contrôlé 28 JUIN 1939

Ce Pedigree est sans valeur officielle s'il n'est revêtu du visa de la Société Centrale et du Nº d'inscription au Livre d'Origines (L. O. F.).

109

that is not one of our cats. I am actually happy that Nicolas chased that one, because that cat is a troublemaker." I could not see any difference between that cat and the hotel cats, but Nicolas could. For the rest of our stay he was the defender of the hotel and its six cats. I was awed anew at the intelligence of my sweet Nicolas.

When the Germans took control of France in 1940, it became very difficult for anyone to own a dog. Life became harder for both Nicolas and me.

To begin with, only doctors and civil servants were given a very limited number of gallons of gas per week. The rest of the population had to do without. We lived in an area of Cavalaire-sur-mer that was quite a distance from the village and shopping center. Getting to the village to buy food became my biggest challenge.

I decided to buy a bicycle and teach Nicolas to sit in a basket attached to the back seat. I stood the bicycle upright, leaning it against a post, and then I tried as best as I could to lift Nicolas and put him into the basket. Since he weighed about thirty pounds, this was a monumental task: I had to get him into the basket and balance the bicycle while I got on it myself. The minute I started to pedal the bicycle, though, Nicolas jumped out. This method of transportation was beneath his dignity!

Again, I went through the task of balancing the bicycle, lifting Nicolas and starting, only to have him jump out again. Finally, exhausted, I gave up. Nicolas would not ride in the basket. However, I had to get to the village. What to do?

"OK, Nicolas," I said to him. "Since you will not ride in the basket, you will have to run alongside my bicycle. So I tried pedaling with Nicolas running beside me. That did not work; he ran at a snail's pace. I could not go more than a mile or so without tiring him.

Finally I told him, "Since you are a slow poke, you leave me no choice but to leave you behind while I go to market." Although he was not happy with this arrangement, Nicolas had to stay home while I rode the bicycle to the market.

From 1940 to 1943, the Italians occupied the area of France in which I lived and were friendly to the French citizens. Some of the soldiers had had enough of the war and Hitler and wanted to hear the truth about what was going on in the world. I became friendly with a few, so much that I could trust them enough to have them to my house. This also gave me an opportunity to gather information to pass to the underground.

These friends would come to my house in the evening, and we would pull the shades down and close the windows. Then we would listen to Parla Londra, the BBC broadcast on the radio.

One of the officers seemed to like us a lot; therefore, we were able to get some extra food, especially for Nicolas. I never knew whether it was my heart or Nicolas's affection that he wanted to win over; but every day after dinner the officer's orderly would knock on our door. He gave me a respectful military salute and handed me a parcel saying, *"Per 'il signor Nicolas."* I do not believe that the poor man knew that *'il signor Nicolas* was the dog. He most likely wondered what kind of presents his superior was sending this mysterious signor Nicolas.

Through the underground I learned about events taking place in France. For example, there was a community of French protestants that lived in the village of Le Chambon-sur-Lignon in the mountains near Vichy. Since 1940 they had been helping and hiding Jews. This was organized mostly by Pastor André Trocmé and his wife Magda. But in 1942 the French police went to the village to stop the assistance to the Jewish people. As a result Pastor Trocmé gave a stirring sermon in his church, urging the people to continue. This resulted in his arrest in February 1943. Later he was released and joined the underground. By the end of the war his efforts saved about 5000 people, of which 3500 were Jewish. These stories were an inspiration to those in the resistance, especially the support from non-Jewish people, but they also added to the stress we felt and the fear of getting caught.

The stress of the occupation was taking its toll on everyone, not just the people involved in the underground and resistance movement. We all lived in fear much of the time and worried about whether or not we would be able to find food. Indeed, it did become more difficult to get food, especially meat. The gravity of the situation weighed heavily on my heart. I worried more about Nicolas than myself, so one day I decided to give him vegetables to help him survive. Nicolas turned his nose up and did not want to eat the vegetables.

I told him, "*Nicolas, ce sont des légumes délicieuses. C'est bon pour toi, mange-les* (Nicolas, these are very delicious vegetables. They are good for you. Eat them)."

I will never forget the look on his face when I pushed the dish of vegetables closer to his face. He looked at me as though I had lost my mind and I could see him thinking, "Aren't these humans stupid, trying to tell us dogs what is good or bad to eat, as if I didn't know right away with one sniff. However, my mistress is a good old soul and I am going to eat them to please her. Besides, I am very hungry. If only I could have bread, nice and crusty, the kind I adore instead of these yucky vegetables!"

Sadly, by this time even bread had been rationed. Each person could only get a very small portion each day with a coupon. I shared my portion with Nicolas, but we were both hungry.

The war dragged on, month by month, year by year. Food became very difficult to obtain and many dogs died of starvation. It was a terrible sight to see them roam the streets, emaciated, hollow eyed, begging for help. My heart broke knowing that there was nothing I could do, that they were doomed. Often after seeing one of these dogs, I would hold Nicolas in my arms and sob quietly, never wanting to think that it might happen to him, and determined that it would not.

Then it seemed as though a miracle happened. The Kennel Club decided that it was important to preserve purebred dogs for post-war France. They wanted to save a few specimens of each breed. If they decided that a specimen was good (deemed worth saving) they would issue ration coupons for the dog to receive five pounds of biscuits every month. Of course, the dog's owner had to pay a high price for them and the Kennel Club was only interested in the dog's physical appearance, not their personality—the part that makes them special, their inner quality.

Hopeful, I took Nicolas to the Kennel Club office in Marseille. It is hard to explain how stressful this visit was for me. I trembled as I walked through the door. I prayed that Nicolas would not sense my fear and anguish. The decision of the Kennel Club representative could mean food or no food, life or death for Nicolas.

When the Kennel Club representative saw Nicolas, his face lit up and he almost gasped. "What a dog! What a beautiful specimen!" he exclaimed.

I was issued a coupon on the spot. My voice qua-
vered and tears formed in my eyes as I thanked
him profusely. They were tears of joy. My wonderful Nicolas would live. I realized that my eye for
beauty, what made me pick him as a puppy, had
probably saved his life.

I took Nicolas and my bag of biscuits home, feeling very proud of my beautiful dog. I set the bag on
the table, anticipating a nice meal for Nicolas. But
when I opened the bag, I almost gagged from the
overpowering, horrible odor. Besides their terrible
smell, the biscuits were hard as nails. It was beyond
my comprehension how a dog could eat, let alone
digest them. They certainly were not meat, nor dog
food. I would not feed these to Nicolas!

However, in our situation, food of any type was
not to be wasted. What could I do? How could I use
these horrible biscuits to save my dear Nicolas? Then
I remembered that the butcher had chickens. Maybe
I could get some meat from the butcher in exchange
for the biscuits for his chickens.

With high hopes I took the bag of biscuits and
went to the butcher.

"Monsieur" I said. "I have been given these biscuits by the Kennel Club for my dog, but he will not
eat them. I am hoping that, if your chickens will eat
them, we can trade some meat for my dog for the
biscuits."

He opened the bag and exclaimed, "Oh, Madame,

they do smell foul. No wonder your dog will not eat them. But chickens do not have a good sense of smell, so let us try and see."

I said a silent prayer as we walked to the chicken pen; I so wanted the chickens to like the biscuits. We broke one into smaller pieces and tossed them into the chicken pen. To my amazement, the chickens actually squabbled over the biscuits. They loved them!

We came to an agreement that in exchange for the biscuits, the butcher gave me some scraps of meat and bones for Nicolas.

At our first meeting, I thought I saw a "look" in the butcher's eye—the kind of look men give to women that they find attractive. I had seen it before since I had a fit figure as a dancer and was considered good looking. But I was so worried about Nicolas that I paid little mind to it. However, it wasn't long before my arrangement with the butcher became most uncomfortable for me. The butcher liked to make passes at me and would pinch my *derrière*. I dared not tell my husband, and I had no choice but to ignore this and pretend that I did not notice. Nicolas never realized what I put up with for him to have a few extra bones.

Then, in 1943, things got worse. The Italians surrendered and the Germans took over the French Riviera. This meant that I was in an even more dangerous position, since I was involved in the resistance with the French underground. Every day we were on our guard, watching yet trying to act "normal" to avoid suspicion. If the Germans caught us or even suspected that we were part of the resistance, we could be shot on the spot or sent to a concentration camp.

Once, while I was in the village to buy food, I saw the Germans arresting a family. The woman tried to run to save her baby, and I heard the Germans shouting at her to stop. But she was afraid, and I believe that she did not think the Germans would shoot a young woman with a baby in her arms, so she did not stop. Next, I heard shots, screaming and then wailing. It seemed there was nothing the Nazis would not do.

On a very nice, sunny October afternoon, I was sitting in my house, playing with Nicolas, when I heard German voices and then my front door banged open. My heart stopped. I thought quickly about running away. But I could not run and leave Nicolas for fear that, if it was the Gestapo, they would shoot him in anger. My husband was not at home. He had often been away lately. He was a very nervous man and fearful of the Germans. Maybe this was not as bad as it seemed, but I realized my worst fears as two Gestapo police officers came and ordered me to follow them.

I cannot adequately explain how awful I felt or the fear that gripped my soul. My heart raced and it felt as though I could not breathe. Where we lived was isolated, and I was alone in the house. My first thought was about Nicolas. Who would take care of him? In desperation I ignored the Gestapo, grabbed Nicolas and started to run to my neighbor's house, about two hundred yards away.

I thought they might be able to take care of him. I had only gone a few feet when I heard a very guttural voice demand, "One more step and we fire!" I heard the Germans release the safeties of their rifles. I knew they would not hesitate to shoot me.

I put Nicolas down in my garden and returned to the house. The Nazis must have thought I would be difficult to handle; they put handcuffs on me and then forced me to get into their car. My mind was racing: *What will happen to Nicolas? Did the Germans find out that I am part of the resistance? What about my husband? Where is he? How will he know where I am? Will he be able to take care of Nicolas?*

The soldiers drove me to the German headquarters and left me there for several hours under guard. Rather than fear for my life, or fear being sent to a concentration camp, all I could think of was Nicolas. As I sat there, I started to talk to two of the men. I had tears in my eyes as I told them about Nicolas. I described him, where I lived, how I had seen starving dogs in the streets and was so afraid that he would die. One of the guards was sympathetic, explaining that he was a dog lover and knew how I felt. He promised to go and care for Nicolas, and if I did not return, to keep him.

Although it broke my heart to think of losing Nicolas, of possibly never seeing him again, I knew that if this German kept his word, my dog would live. That gave me hope for Nicolas.

After a few hours, they drove me to a prison in Toulon, fifty miles away. During the day and especially at night, I had nightmares. I would picture Nicolas dead from hunger, or frozen in Russia where the Germans had taken him. One nightmare after another plagued me for the entire time that I was held captive. From the prison in Toulon I was sent to the Austerlitz camp in Paris where I was held for a year and a half.

Then in July 1944, I was shipped with 999 other people to Auschwitz. My hopes of returning home dimmed with each passing day. I had heard rumors about Auschwitz from the underground. I knew that people did not survive this camp.

No one knew how long the war would last. No one had communication with the outside world. My fears increased. I did not know the fate of my husband, only that he had been arrested about the same time as I was. So I knew he would not be there to take care of Nicolas.

Then one of the most glorious days of my life happened. After eighteen horrible months in captivity, I was free! I was alive and was able to go home. I had survived the camps.

Transportation was not reliable and it took me days to get to my home. I had to walk much of the way which, in my weakened state, was a chore. But my hope and desire to find Nicolas drove me on.

Finally I was about a mile from my home. As I neared the house, I began to tremble. Would Nicolas be there? Would I find his bones lying in my garden or a poorly marked grave? Had the kind German soldier fetched him and kept him as he promised?

Tears came to my eyes as I opened the door to my house. Softly I called, "Nicolas, Nicolas." Only silence greeted me. I walked outside to the garden where I had last seen him. As carefully as I looked, I could not find a clue as to his whereabouts. All of the horror and tension hit me at once and I slumped down, crying bitter tears, tears of relief that I was home and tears for my poor Nicolas. What would I do now?

As the days wore on, I continued in vain to search for him, to try to find out what happened. My husband was nowhere to be found and I could get no information about him.

As I retraced the steps of my arrest, I learned that the German soldier had come for Nicolas as he had promised. The soldier and the rest of the men in his unit, the Army of the Occupation, adopted

Nicolas. When their battalion left St. Tropez, they took Nicolas with them. As the Allies stormed Pampelone Beach in the South of France, the Germans retreated, and again Nicolas went with them. However, Nicolas's adventures were not over.

About one hundred miles inland in the small village of Sospel, the Germans had to abandon Nicolas. For a few days he wandered about, trying to find food and taking shelter where he could. However, he had been well cared for and fed by the Germans, so he did not look like many of the starving dogs that roamed the streets. By the grace of God, through all of his trials in the two years that we were separated, Nicolas never lost his collar with his nametag. Soon a family from Nice found him, took care of him, and sought to locate me.

One day I received a letter from people that I did not know. I could not imagine who they were and, with some trepidation, tore open the letter. My hands shook and my eyes filled with tears as I stood there reading:

> *Dear M. Rothschild,*
> *We dearly hope that you will receive this letter in good health. I wish to inform you that we have found your dog, Nicolas.*

My heart leapt for joy and I collapsed onto a chair. My dear, dear Nicolas was alive and was found! What joy I felt, what answer to prayer. I thanked God with all my heart.

The letter went on to explain where Nicolas was and how to make arrangements to get him. I quickly wrote back and rushed the letter to the post.

So, in 1945, Nicolas and I were reunited. The family in Nice had agreed to bring him to me. I waited at the door, watching for them. I imagined Nicolas jumping for joy when he saw me, running into my arms and showering me with kisses.

When the family from Nice arrived, though, Nicolas was not overwhelmed to see me! What a disappointment; but I was too overjoyed to be hurt.

He left his temporary family with an air of indifference; he had become quite the self-sufficient little man. I always felt that he was angry with me for leaving him. The war had changed all of us forever, and Nicolas was no exception. However, our adventures were still not over.

My father and mother lived in California, and for personal and important reasons, I decided to move there. I still lived in fear of retribution for being in the resistance, and I suspected that my husband had turned me in to save himself, although I had no proof of that assumption.

However, during 1945 in Europe, civilians who needed to travel found it very difficult, if not impossible; and a dog was almost out of the question. Nevertheless, I was not going to leave Nicolas again, not after all we had been through together. I was determined that we would both go to California.

Before I could get all of the arrangements made, a friend invited Nicolas and me to come and stay for a rest. She had a lovely old house in Normandy. She also had a mixed Labrador retriever named Cambouis, who was very friendly. Although I was home and relatively safe, I dearly needed a rest and the company of a friend. My home held unpleasant memories, and I thought it would be good for Nicolas and me to get away.

When we arrived, my friend's dog rushed out to greet us enthusiastically. Nicolas just stood there, sniffing Cambouis and regarding him. To say that Nicolas was a bit reserved is an understatement.

It did not take long, though, for the two to become fast friends, to the point where they plotted against us humans! This happened within an hour or so of them meeting. I can only imagine what thoughts and communications these two had in that first hour. Both dogs—well trained, mannerly and a delight to live with—almost instantly became brats!

Obedience was now a forgotten word and they organized their lives exactly the way they wanted, and to heck with the humans. We knew it would be a temporary situation and put up with their antics. Otherwise we would have had to intervene.

Since Nicolas and I had just been reunited, I did not want to correct him; I was not sure how he had been treated. And, after the terrible war years, my friend and I felt that this should be a time of relaxation for everyone; so we made a real holiday of our time together.

Because of Normandy's very damp climate, I had prepared a soft, comfortable bed for Nicolas in the warmest room of the house, the kitchen.

The old coal stove burned all through the day and even into the night. Cambouis also had a bed in the kitchen where he had slept for years. His bed was large to accommodate his large frame.

During the night, after we had all retired to our sleeping quarters, I could not sleep. I guess I was still suffering from the trials I had experienced, as lights, noises and dreams continued to plague me. And I had been so obsessed with worrying about and then finding Nicolas that I now wanted to reassure myself that he was still in the house and okay.

So I crept to the kitchen and peeked in. To my amazement, there was Nicolas, stretched out on Cambouis's large bed. Poor Cambouis had tried to curl up on Nicolas's bed, which was so small that half of his body was resting on the cold floor. I went in and made the dogs change beds, thinking that they did not understand to which bed each of them belonged. Before I could walk back out the kitchen door, they had changed back again, Nicolas on Cambouis's bed and Cambouis on Nicolas's bed. They both looked tolerantly at me as if I were some sort of a moron.

Their expression clearly said, "You poor fool, can't you see that this is the way we like it? What does it matter to you how and where we sleep? Please leave us alone." What could I do but leave the two stubborn dogs in their uncomfortable positions?

Now I want to explain that before we arrived at my friend's home, Cambouis followed a regular routine. Before eight o'clock in the morning, he would start his watchdog duties by barking, announcing the arrival of the milkman. However, that first morning was silent—no barking from Cambouis. My friend was surprised and asked the maid what was going on. "Madame," said the maid. "The dogs are still in bed and refuse to get up!"

Around nine o'clock these two men of leisure yawned, stretched and went into the garden to start their day. Not once during our stay did these two beasts start their watchdog service before nine o'clock in the morning. After that hour, they were alert and barked at every intruder. They must have joined a canine union that gave them most definite orders not to start work early so that they would not exert themselves. Each day the maid would report to us in a desolate tone of voice as she served our breakfast, "The dogs are *still* asleep." We always had a chuckle over it.

What puzzled us every day was that Nicolas was always damp, as if he had run under the sprinklers, even when there were no sprinklers on. Finally, we discovered the cause. Cambouis licked Nicolas from head to toe a few times a day. We never could stop it or understand the reason for it. Both dogs seemed to consider this ritual washing a very important part of their daily routine.

When we had dinner, against all good principles, we allowed both dogs in the dining room while we ate. Cambouis only had to put his head on the table to beg for food. To get rid of him we had to give him a tidbit. Nicolas of course could not reach the table in this manner, but he quickly learned that if he got on his hind legs, put his paws and big head on the table, then he got his tidbit. The two of them were so funny that we could not be angry with them. We also kept in mind that this behavior was only going to last for a short time, since I would be leaving and both dogs would then behave as they should.

Time seemed to fly by while I visited in Normandy and it was still necessary to solve the problem of getting Nicolas to America. I was offered a seat on an airplane that was leaving from England. This presented a problem since England had a strict quarantine for animals. Therefore, Nicolas could not fly with me. The problem seemed insurmountable since I flatly refused to leave Nicolas behind. What was I to do?

I was feeling very depressed and hopeless when another miracle occurred in my life.

When all seemed lost, a couple that I knew who

were dog lovers, offered to take Nicolas with them on their trip to America via a Liberty ship. Nicolas had the royal treatment on his trip; he was not confined to a kennel but given the free run of the ship. He landed in New York, then flew to Hollywood.

When he arrived in Hollywood, he created quite a stir among dog lovers. His fame spread because he had been a prisoner of war. He was photographed, interviewed (I answered for him), was featured on the front page of the newspapers and for a few days was a real celebrity. Of course, he took all of this in stride, enjoyed the sun, the lawns, and the good food; and he ignored the compliments paid to him by all of his admirers.

He always had been very sure of himself, not exuberant but rather serious, not too friendly and with a strong personality that affirmed itself more and more. But this is what I loved about Nicolas. He was a real character.

After almost two years in California, Nicolas's health started to fail. I took him to the best veterinarians available and cared for him exactly the way they instructed me. I could not bear the thought of losing my beloved companion after all we had been through. It did not seem fair—after all, he had barely had time to enjoy his good life in California. Alas, as much as I tried, he died just before his ninth birthday. I was heartbroken and could not be consoled. I agonized and went over everything in my mind. Could I have done more? Was it the hardship of the war? Was it the long trip from France to America? Or was he destined to a short life like his father and other members of his line?

He and I had been through so much together, more than any dog or person should have to go through in one lifetime. He had been a great little dog, and I loved him. He had an extraordinary life. If only I could have kept him forever.

There were more French bulldogs in my life, but never another Nicolas. I am glad I could share my life with him.

7. YUGOSLAVIA

*O*n *April 6, 1941, a combination of German, Italian, Hungarian and Bulgarian forces attacked Yugoslavia. By April 17 the various regions of the Yugoslavia government signed an armistice with Germany and more than three hundred thousand Yugoslav officers and soldiers were taken prisoner.*

Yugoslavia was split into sections; two (Croatia and a Serbian state) became puppets of the Nazis, ruled by a fascist militia known as the Ustaše. The rest of the country was divided between Bulgaria, Hungry and Italy.

The concentration camp Jasenovac was created in the Independent State of Croatia and a large number of men, women and children, mostly Serbs, were executed there.

Just as in other countries across Europe, the Yugoslavs who opposed the Nazis organized a resistance movement. This turned out to be the largest resistance army in occupied Western and Central Europe. The guerrilla activities of this army were very effective. So much so that the Germans retaliated by executing one hundred civilians for every German soldier killed and fifty civilians killed for every soldier wounded.

During WWII, the island of Korcula along with most of Dalmatia was given to the Italians. After the armistice between Italy and the Allied powers in 1943, this area was briefly controlled by the Yugoslav partisans, but then occupied by the Germans until it was liberated in 1944.

Dolly

by Sonja Alaimo

For me, life was good in Zagreb, Yugoslavia; but then, at nine years of age, I was not burdened by the necessities of life. However, even at that young age, I had a great love of animals.

One day, while I was outside, I heard an awful screaming. I went to see what it was and saw a man trying to kill a piglet. I was sickened at the sight because the man was not very good at it and the piglet escaped from him. It ran away screaming, which is what I heard. This caused me to become very upset because I loved all animals. After witnessing this, thereafter I refused to eat meat and I felt even more sympathy for animals.

My parents and I lived in an apartment near my grandparents. I loved my grandmother, and we often visited or went for walks together.

One day my mother surprised me with a wire-haired fox terrier puppy named Dolly. She was about six months old when she came into my life. Dolly had a bouncy, crisp nature about her that, I learned later, is common with fox terriers. She was quick and alert, and very smart. She learned her lessons well and was eager to please me. Dolly became my most devoted playmate. She watched me from our balcony as I roller-skated or rode my bicycle.

My mother told me that, during the day while I was in school, Dolly would anxiously wait for me to come home. Dolly would pace for a while, and then she would lie down or sit and watch the door. Sometimes she would whimper. If she heard something that sounded like me coming, she would raise her head and ears and look intently, waiting. She knew the time I was due home, and at that time she became very alert. When I finally did arrive home, she would jump as high as my head and give me kisses all over.

This feeling of waiting was mutual because, even though I paid attention in school, I too would often think of Dolly and look forward to going home to be with her.

My grandmother, Dolly and I would go for walks in the park. Sometimes I would duck behind a tree or a bush and hide from Dolly. Then she would search for me and find me. We played hide-and-seek this way many times. I was never able to evade Dolly's keen nose. Other times I would throw a ball and Dolly would gleefully run after it and bring it back. However, there were the quiet times too, when Dolly, my grandmother and I would sit enjoying the grass, trees and flowers in the park. Dolly always enjoyed

watching the birds and squirrels that lived there. Grandmother and I would have "serious" talks about anything that came to mind.

Going to bed each night involved a ritual. I would select one of my old blouses and put it on Dolly. I know now that she must have looked funny in frills, but I thought she looked beautiful. I did this so that she would not get cold. Dolly seemed to love sleeping in my blouse. When I climbed into bed, Dolly would jump up and curl herself into a small ball at the foot of the bed, always touching my feet.

I was not aware of the world situation and the beginnings of World War II. Even though I had heard some talk about it, my parents tried to shield me from the horrors that were brewing.

Quite suddenly the Germans attacked Yugoslavia. My family had only a few days to escape to the Dalmatian coast; we could only take a few personal possessions. One of the things I took was a photo that included Dolly.

My father had escaped a week before we did. During the week he was gone, my mother managed to get false papers for her and me. A man came from the Croatian coast and pretended to be my father so that he could escort us to safety. We had to travel by railroad.

My mother arranged for a friend that she trusted to take Dolly. The friend walked with us to the railroad station, with Dolly on a leash.

With tears running down my cheeks, I begged my mother, "Please, can we take Dolly? I promise to take care of her. She will not understand why we are leaving her and her heart will break."

My mother was stressed and trying to be strong. "Sonja, you must understand, we cannot take Dolly with us. She will be fine. We will get her when we can."

As my mother tried to comfort me, Dolly was equally upset, pulling, and straining on her leash to get to me. I thought I could hear her crying too.

"Mama, Mama, please," I cried. "Can't we take Dolly too?" I begged again. How my heart was breaking. My mother turned away to hide her tears as she escorted me onto the train. I kept looking for Dolly as we boarded the train and I strained to see her as the train pulled away. I watched Dolly for as long as I could, and she kept her sight on the train.

I did not fully understand at the time how very upset my mother was. She loved Dolly too, but we were traveling with false papers, and my mother was terrified that we would be discovered. This was her main concern. My mother realized that if we were discovered it would mean a concentration camp and most likely death.

What I did not realize at the time was that the Italian army was locating several hundred families on the islands. My family was sent to Korcula where we were reunited with my father. This is where we spent the entire war.

Life was not easy on this island; we lived in fear that at any time the Germans would come marching in and discover us. And there was always a shortage of food.

One of the most difficult things that we had to face was that we had no contact with the outside world. Dolly and my grandmother were always on my mind. I prayed that they would be there when we returned. I wanted to live as we did before. I longed for the walks in the park with Grandmother and Dolly. I wanted to see my friends again.

On the plus side, we were not forced into slave labor. There were many professors on the island, so the families got together and formed schools for the children. I learned to speak six languages, and to draw and paint in addition to the standard studies.

There was an Italian commander in charge of the island. He was a kind man and cared for his charges. When the United States and British armies liberated Italy, the Italian commander allowed anyone who wanted, to go with him to Italy. He would not abandon the people who were exiled to the island. My family went to Italy where we lived for six years.

Meanwhile, when the war was over, my mother contacted our home in Yugoslavia. She found out that shortly after we left, my grandmother had died. True to her promise to me years ago, my mother continued to try to find out if Dolly was still alive and waiting for us.

But, finally, we learned that Dolly also had died.

Dolly could not understand why her life was torn apart. She had never been away from Sonja, except when she left for school. However, Dolly sensed that this was different. Though she did not understand why, she knew that her beloved companion was very upset.

As the train pulled out of the station, Dolly jumped and yelped. The neighbor, whom she knew, reached down and patted her head and sides, murmuring gentle words of comfort. But that was not the same as Sonja patting her. Dolly gave up trying to run after the train, though she looked back often as she and the neighbor walked to her new home.

As the days wore on, Dolly did not accept her fate. She would pace and whimper softly, longing for Sonja and her family. When the neighbor took her for walks in the park, she would pull to go to the familiar places, hoping that Sonja and Grandmother would be there waiting, playing one of their hiding games. But alas, they never were.

At every chance she got, Dolly would run back to "her" apartment and sit on the steps, watching for Sonja to come home. At the time Sonja would normally come home from school, Dolly would pace

back and forth. At night she wandered restlessly
through the house.

We were told that one day Dolly looked out a second-
story window and saw a girl walking up the street.
She must have thought it was me. Excitedly, Dolly
jumped out of the window to try to get to me.

When my mother told me this, I cried for weeks.
My young heart was so broken, the sadness has
never left me.

We never returned to our home. All of our possessions were sold; there was nothing left to return to.
From Italy we moved to the United States.

Some of the happiest memories of my childhood
are about Dolly and my grandmother. I feel that I
owe my deep fondness for animals to knowing Dolly.

I still have the photo of Dolly, and it is a treasure
to me.

About the Contributors

Sonja Alaimo was a child in Yugoslavia, where her early years were full of promise. With the German invasion, her family escaped to the Dalmation Coast and spent four years of interment on the island of Korcula. Due to negative political developments in Yugoslavia, return was not possible. Hence, Sonja's family went to Italy to work and study and wait departure to the U.S., where they eventually settled in New York City. After a career as a corporate CEO, Sonja retired, and she now paints and sculpts.

Joyce Clemens was born and raised in The Netherlands where dogs are considered to be members of the family, are taught good manners and are welcomed in restaurants, theaters and department stores. Joyce and her husband moved to Georgia in the 1970s. After their sons were grown, Joyce made dog training her career, becoming certified as a Master Obedience Trainer. Using positive reinforcement to train dogs and their companions for a long-lasting partnership is her primary goal. She specializes in psychiatric service dogs, especially important for vets returning from war.

Lya (Leventhal) Galperin was born on February 14, 1931 in Faleshty, Romania. During the war, she and her family were taken to different gettoes in the Ukraine. In May of 1981 they immigrated from the Soviet Union to the U.S. She lives with her son, daughter-in-law and two grandchildren in San Francisco.

Irene Markley was born in 1925 in Munkacs which was then part of Czechoslovakia. In 1938 it became a possession of Hungary. In 1944 the Germans came, and by May of 1944 Munkacs was declared free of Jews, all having been put in a ghetto and sent to Auschwitz. While her family lived in the ghetto, Irene escaped two times, finally reaching Budapest where she lived under a Christian name, as did her brother and one sister. Her parents and other sisters died in Auschwitz. Irene met her future husband in 1945 in her home town and they were married that year. In 1949 after living in Displaced Person's (DP) camps, she and her husband moved to the United States.

Kurt Moses survived the Holocaust, married Doris Rothschild in 1955, and they had two daughters, Wendy and Michelle. Kurt settled in Harrisburg, PA. During the Holocaust, he was separated from his family by the Nazis in 1942 and sent to two concentration camps and then finally to Auschwitz until 1945. His father was killed at Birkenau. Then in 1947, with the help of an uncle, he was reunited with his mother and sister in New York. Despite the horrors and nightmares that he suffered during the Holocaust, Kurt overcame, becoming a renowned speaker, lecturer and mentor for many people. His life story is one of courage and triumph over fear and hatred.

Yvonne Redgis was born in France to an American father and a French mother. She was living on the Riviera when she was arrested in 1943 for anti-German activities, and was deported to Auschwitz. Surviving the concentration camp, after the war she immigrated to the U.S., where she developed notoriety as a popular, vivacious speaker.

Annette Renschowicz is a daughter of Holocaust survivors from Poland. She was born and raised in New York City. She worked for the NYC Department of Education as a teacher's assistant for children of special needs. Annette loves to travel. On a trip to Israel, a family member related to her the narrative of her grandfather's dog. She then journeyed to her parents' former shtetl and the concentration camps in Poland. She is a strong advocate for protecting stray animals. She currently lives with her companion of twenty-nine years, Raphael, and her cat, Penelope, in Brooklyn.

Gloria Rubin was a child in Poland, where her father had a wheat mill and her parents took in girls from a nearby orphanage. In 1939 the family were taken to the Warsaw ghetto. Gloria was the only one of her family to survive the Holocaust.

 Kathy Rubin was fifteen years old at the end of World War II. She had been in Teresienstadt, Czechoslovakia with her mother and three siblings, and all of them returned to Hungary. When they arrived at their home, they happily found that her father had also survived the war. In 1956 Kathy married, and a few months later the couple escaped from Hungary during The Hungarian Uprising. They made their way to the U.S. They had two children and many family pets, including cats, a dog, goldfish, chickens and ducks. Kathy now enjoys gardening, going on cruises, attending lectures and helping people.

Jacob Stern and his family tried to flee on foot from the Nazis but were caught and sent to a concentration camp. Fortunately, his family—parents, brother and sister—all survived.

Sources Consulted

The Holocaust Chronicle, Publications International, Ltd., (2000), IL.

Keegan, John, (1989), *The Second World War*, Viking Penguin, NY.

Matanle, Ivor, (1998), *World War II*, Smithmark Publishers, NY.

Moses, Kurt, (2005), *Home At Last: Auschwitz Survivor: A Memoir*, Martell Publishing, Inc., San Diego, CA.

North, Oliver, (2005), *War Stories III: The Heroes Who Defeated Hitler*, Regnery Publishing Inc., Washington, DC.

Shirer, William L., (1969), *The Collapse of the Third Republic, An Inquiry into the Fall of France in 1940*, Simon & Schuster, NY.

Sulzberger, C.L. (1966), *American Heritage Picture History of World War II*, American Heritage Publishing Company, NY.

Index

André Trocmé, Pastor, 112
Anthony McAuliffe, General
refusal to surrender, 63
Armia Krajowa
part of Polish resistance, 42
Battle of Ardennes (in Belgium), 63
Arrow Cross Party, 17
BBC radio broadcast, 111
Josephine Baker
performances in France, 104
Battle of Bastogne (in Belgium), 63
boîte in the rue Volney
the arts in France, 104
Battle of the Bulge, 63
Battle of Norway (in Poland), 41
Battle of Uman
Hungarian Army success, 16
Baty (playwrite), 104
Béla Imrédy
Hungary prime minister, 16
Henri Bernstein (playwrite), 104
Léon Blum (president of France), 104
Lucienne Boyer (French singer), 104
Brussels
hiding from Germans in, 65
Budapest (Hungary)
living there under Christian name, 35, 39
Cavalaire-sur-mer (France), 103, 110
Casino de Paris
Maurice Chevalier performed there, 104
Josephine Baker performed there, 104

Constanta
coastal city in Romania, 95
Croatia
independent state of, 129
Czestochowa
city in Poland, 43-45
Dalmatia
given to Italy, 129
escape to coast, 133
Diary of Anne Frank
kept pet cat in hiding, 10
risk of death to hide Jews, 68
Don River
Hungarian Army there, 16
Drente (Holland), 77
Dutch
involvement in WWII, 67-68
air attack by Germans, 73
railway strike, 68, 82
Elvire (play), 104
French
protestants in Le Chambon
helped and hid Jews, 112
underground, 105, 111-119
German occupation of, 121
Gawlova (Poland), 51
Geleen (Holland), 73
German
invasion of Netherlands, 73
Gyula Gömbös
Hungary prime minister, 16

Hajduhadhaz (Hungary), 20, 23
Hongerwinter, 68
Hungarian
  government, 16-17
  army, 16 17
  police, 17
  Jews, 17
Hunger Winter, 68, 82
Iron Guard (in Romania), 88
Israel
  proclaimed state, 14
  moved there after war, 49
  award given to non-Jews by, 102
István Bethlen, Count
  regime in Hungary, 16
Jasenovac (Croatia)
  concentration camp, 129
Jew Laws, 74
JOINT (Jewish organization), 95-96
Korcula, island of, 129, 134
Le Chambon-sur-Lignon
  where French Protestant Christians
  sheltered Jews, 112
Le Matin (Paris newspaper), 103
Liberty ship
  to America, 127
Lublin (Poland)
  herded in cattle cars to, 53
Mengele, Dr., 79
Munkacs (Hungary), 32
Narodowe Sily Zbrojne
  Polish underground force, 42
Normandy
  invasion of, 68
  house in, 123
  climate of, 124
Novemiasto ghetto, 60-61
Nuts!, 63

onderduikers
  Dutch participants in underground
  resistance movement, 68
Operation Margarethe
  German march into and
  occupation of Hungary, 17
Orphanage
  Polish (in Nasielsk), 51
  Soviet, 99
Pál Teleki, Count
  prime minister Hungary, 16
Palestine
  offer of going to, 95-96
Parla Londra
  BBC radio broadcast, 111
Phony War (France), 102
Polish
  Highland Brigade, 41
  resistance, 41-42
  underground, 42, 54
Pampelone Beach (France), 121
Second Infantry Fusiliers (Poland), 41
Serbian state, 129
shtetle, 89
Sittard (Holland), 69-70, 75, 80
Sospel (France), 121
St. Tropez (France), 103, 121
stock market crash (1929)
  Holland suffered from, 67
Theresienstadt (Czechoslovakia)
  Jews sent there, 26, 78, 80
Ustaše fascist militia, 129
Vichy (France), 102, 112
Westerbork concentration camp in
  Holland, 77-78
Zagreb (Yugoslavia), 130

About the Author/Compiler

 **Susan Bulanda**, a recognized and accomplished dog trainer since 1963, has worked with many dogs in a variety of fields, including worldwide expertise in canine Search & Rescue (SAR).

Her certifications and consulting in animal behavior include both dogs and cats. Her wealth of knowledge supported her contributions to the International Association of Animal Behavior Consultants both as vice president and dog chairperson. A key contributor to the advisory committee of the National Search Dog Alliance, she has formed and run two canine SAR units and worked as a judge in England's First and Second International Canine SAR Competitions. Susan is a retired senior conformation judge for the United Kennel Club and has shown a variety of breeds in the conformation ring.

Ms. Bulanda holds a B.A. in Psychology and a M.A. in Education. As an Adjunct Professor at Kutztown University, she developed two Canine Training and Management programs.

Ms. Bulanda's award-winning articles include "Dogdom's Moral Show Down" (*Dog World Magazine*) co-written with Larry Shook, and "Life and Death, When It's All Up to You and Your Dog" (*Good Dog Magazine*). She received the Freedom Foundation's George Washington Medal of Honor and holds a patent for the training and use of mold detection dogs.

An award-winning author, Susan has lectured worldwide, written hundreds of articles, and penned the book, *God's Creatures: A Biblical View of Animals* (Cladach), as well as *READY!: The Training of the Search and Rescue Dog, Ready to Serve, Ready to Save: Strategies of Real Life Search and Rescue Missions, Scenting on the Wind: Scent Work for Hunting Dogs, Boston Terriers: Complete Pet Owner's Manual*, and *The Canine Source Book*.

Ms. Bulanda and her husband, Larry, reside in Maryland.

Also by Susan Bulanda

GOD'S CREATURES
A Biblical View of Animals

Animal lovers who are curious to know
how the Scriptures address animal
issues, will find plenty in this book to
inform and delight.

CPSIA information can be obtained
at www.ICGtesting.com
Printed in the USA
LVOW04s1528020816
498752LV00001B/43/P